BASEBALL HAS DONE IT

Copyright ©2005 by Rachel Robinson
Originally published in 1964.

ISBN: 0-9752517-2-4
ISBN: 9780975251720

Ig Publishing
178 Clinton Avenue
Brooklyn, New York 11205

www.igpub.com

Distributed in the United States and Canada
by Consortium Book Sales & Distribution
1045 Westgate Drive, Suite 90
Saint Paul, Minnesota 55114-1065

Cover design by Pure + Applied
Text design by Dayna Navaro

Library of Congress Cataloging-in-Publication Data

Robinson, Jackie, 1919-1972.
  Baseball has done it / Jackie Robinson with an introduction by Spike Lee.
      p. cm.
  Originally published: Philadelphia : Lippincott, 1964.
  ISBN 0-9752517-2-4 (alk. paper)
1. Robinson, Jackie, 1919-1972. 2. Baseball players--United States--Biography.
3. African American baseball players--Biography. 4. Discrimination in sports--
United States--History--20th century. I. Title.
  GV865.R6A2 2005
  796.357'092--dc22

                          2005003709

Printed in Canada

BASEBALL HAS DONE IT

Jackie Robinson

With an Introduction by Spike Lee

PUBLISHING

Brooklyn, New York

BASEBALL HAS DONE IT

Introduction

*A*s far back as I can remember, Jackie Robinson has been an inspiration in my life. If you were a kid like me, growing up in Brooklyn in the 1960s, there was no figure more revered than Jackie Robinson. Jackie was spoken of with the same sense of respect and awe as Dr. King, as Joe Louis, as Jesus Christ.

To get an understanding of Jackie's importance to my generation, you have to realize what a different world I came out of, and of the importance of sports to that world. Forty odd years ago, (I was born in 1957) there were no such things as video games to keep kids occupied. But, we had better than video games—we had sports and our imaginations. Winter, spring, summer, fall, sports was our world. Since we didn't have organized Little League teams, we would make up our own "official" schedules, like in the Major Leagues, but instead of one team against another, it was one street against the other. We played the usual sports, baseball, football, basketball, as well as a variety of "street" games that are nearly forgotten today, games like Down the Sewer, Chinese Handball, Booties Up (if you lost, they threw a ball at your ass), stickball and Johnny on the Pony.

Being passionate sports fan, we all had our own individual heroes. Some kids liked Mickey Mantle. Some liked Willie Mays. (Which lead to many an argument—I was a Mays man.) My big heroes, however, courteousy of Roger Kahn's *The Boys of Summer*, were the great Brooklyn Dodger teams of the 1950s. The teams of Jackie Robinson, Roy Campanella, Don Newcombe, Preacher Roe, Carl Erskine, Clem Labine, Pee Wee Reese, Joe Black, Jim Gilliam. These men were the heroes of my youth, and, as an adult, I have been lucky to not only meet many of these players, but also become good friends with some of them, especially the late Joe Black, and Don Newcombe, who I still check in on whenever I am out in California. And while I never got to know Jackie Robinson (I only met him once, when I was a boy), I am fortunate to have become friends with his lovely widow, Rachel, who has gone on to do great work with the Jackie Robinson Foundation, sending thousands of intelligent, but financially needy kids to school.

Sadly, these heroes of my youth have been forgotten by today's youth. And it is not only African American sports heroes like Jackie Robinson—the kids of today don't even know who JFK was, or Martin Luther King. Sure, they may have heard of JFK, or heard of Martin Luther King, but whatever knowledge they have is superficial—all they know about Dr. King is that they get a day off from school on his birthday. It is the same with Jackie Robinson—they may know he was the first African-American baseball player, but beyond that, nothing. Nothing about the importance of his accomplisments, about his sacrifices, and the meaning of those sacrifices. There has been a total breakdown as far as history is concerned in this country, and young people today have no interest in anything that happened before they were born. And that's a tragedy.

Even today's black athletes, whose livelihoods are the direct result of sacrifices of men like Jackie Robinson, have forgotten. Remember Vince Coleman, who played with the Cardinals in the 1980s and 1990s, saying, "Who's Jackie Robinson?" Today's African-American athletes owe everything to Jackie Robinson, and to others like him, such as Jesse Owens, such as Joe Louis, such as Curt Flood, who sacrificed his career, sacrificed his life, in challenging the reserve clause in baseball. If it weren't for people like Curt Flood, and Jackie, and Jesse, and Joe, the athletes of today wouldn't be making the kind of money they're making. Unfortunately, the only thing that matters to today's players is getting paid. They're not educated about the past, so their level of consciousness is not high. They know nothing of the many African-American athletes who put their careers on the line to fight for future generations, men like John Carlos, Tommy Smith, Mohammed Ali, Jackie, Jim Brown, Kareem Abdul Jabbar, Bill Russell. We can't forget these people, can't forget their stories—they are great American stories.

This book is about baseball and integration, and the progress that had been made up until 1964, almost twenty years after Jackie broke the color line. In the book, Jackie is optimistic about the future, saying, "if baseball can do it, so can the rest of society," Yet, I think if Jackie were alive today, he would be disappointed with how things have gone with baseball and integration. Take a look at Major League front offices—there are no black owners, and only one black GM. Take a look at the players—the number of African-American players has declined over the past several years. There are several reasons for that. One is that African-American kids today are into other sports, specifically basketball and football. Also, I believe that white owners would rather deal with Latino players instead of black players because Latinos, especially those from the Dominican Republic, are desperate, because of their poverty, to get off that island, so that will take a lot more abuse than African-Americans will. So, the cycle of discrimination continues, with African-American athletes getting the short end, again.

Because of all of this, it is more important than ever to remember Jackie Robinson. Even though he has been celebrated over the years, I think that people still don't understand how immense Jackie's heart was. What he did had to be one of the most heroic things known to man. One of the hardest things to do in sports is to hit major league pitching, but to do that, with the entire weight of your race on your shoulders, while being ridiculed, lambasted, having racial epithets hurled at you, and not being able to say anything back, as Branch Rickey ordered Jackie to do for his rookie year, to go through all of that, and still perform at a high level, is one of the great American stories. So, in honor of Jackie, and many other African-American heroes, some remembered, many forgotten, we got to keep fighting hard, keep whacking away, so as not to let the flames blow out. That is the only way to celebrate Jackie Robinson.

—Spike Lee

Jackie Robinson, Joe Louis and Mohammed Ali.
Photo courtesy of Jackie Robinson Archive

BASEBALL HAS DONE IT

PART I

The Past

1

The right of every American to first-class citizenship is the most important issue today.

We Negroes are determined that our children shall enjoy the same blessings of democracy as white children. We are adamant: we intend to use every means at our disposal to smash segregation and discrimination wherever it appears. We are staring into the face of our oppressors and demanding by what right of skin coloration do they consider themselves our superiors.

We have no illusions about the difficulties that lie ahead. We clearly understand that the falsehoods about our supposed inferiority have taken deep root in the minds of white Americans. These lies are now being exposed for what they are. They must be totally destroyed.

In 1954 I boarded a plane with an umpire who had known me eight years earlier as a rookie in the International League. At that time I was following Branch Rickey's wise advice to turn the other cheek to provocations. By 1949 I was established as a big-leaguer, and Mr. Rickey said, "You've earned the right to be yourself, Jackie. You've given so much to the game that you are now in a position to comport yourself as other players do. You're on your own now."

From that moment I defended myself against anti-Negro insults with all the force at my command.

Now in 1954 this umpire, sitting beside me in the plane, asked, "What's made you change your attitude, Jackie? I liked you much better when you were less aggressive."

"I'm not concerned with your liking or disliking me," I retorted.

"All I ask is that you respect me as a human being." I explained that I was proud to be a Negro. I said God had given us certain unique qualities, that we cherish our heritage just as Englishmen, Frenchmen, Jews, Indians and every other group of common origin cherish theirs. "I am not ashamed of my dark skin," I said. "You and every other white American should understand that we believe our color is an asset. Your dislike of my aggressiveness has no effect on me. I'm after something much more important than your favor or disfavor. You should at least admit that you respect me as a man who stands up for what he believes in. I am not an Uncle Tom. I am in this fight to stay."

This incident stands out in my memory among the many that came my way when I was less Jackie Robinson, ball player, than the Negro who had dared invade a popular sport which, until then, had been lily white.

Today Negroes play on every big league club and in every minor league. With millions of other Negroes in other walks of life we are willing to stand up and be counted for what we believe in. In baseball or out we are no longer willing to wait until Judgment Day for equality—we want it here on earth as well as in heaven. We are going to press forward against bigotry until the bigots understand the full meaning of that precious word: democracy. Ladies and gentlemen, we mean what we say when we shout, "Give us freedom!"

This book is not about me, although of necessity I appear in it. Nor is it about baseball as a game of hits, runs and errors. It's about a sociological experiment which has revealed certain truths about human relations, a research laboratory and proving ground for democracy in action. Branch Rickey was the Einstein who provided the magic formula and then applied it, using me and other Negro players as raw material. In these pages he will speak in his own words as will others, including representative baseball executives and players of yesterday and today. The latter will relate their personal experiences as well as their reactions, beliefs and hopes for the future of integration.

For integration has a future today. How bright that future will be depends on the American people as represented by their government in support of civil rights legislation.

As never before, the time is NOW for democracy in action not words.

Integration in baseball has already proved that all Americans can live together in peaceful competition. Negroes and whites coexist today on diamonds South, North,

East and West without friction, fist fights or feuds. They wear the same uniforms, sit side by side on the same benches, use the same water fountains, toilets, showers; the same bats, balls and gloves. They travel from city to city on the same buses, trains or planes. They live in the same hotels, eat in the same dining rooms, kid each other in the same baseball jargon. Negro and white ball players play cards and golf together, go to movies together, swap inside information about opponents, defend each other in rhubarbs, pound each other's backs after a winning game. They attend postseason banquets together, go on club picnics, visit each other's homes. Fans no longer notice the color of a ball player's skin. Willie Mays is San Francisco's hero. Milwaukee fans roar encouragement to Henry Aaron as he goes to the plate. Cincinnati's fans live or die on Frank Robinson's batting average. Now that Stan Musial has retired, Bill White is the most popular Cardinal, as Ernie Banks is the most respected Cub. New York reporters divide their post-game time between the lockers of Mickey Mantle, Whitey Ford, and Elston Howard, quizzing each about the newsier points of the contest just ended. From Boston, where fans mobbed Earl Wilson after his 1962 no-hitter, to Los Angeles, where Tommy Davis is the toast of the town, baseball is an all-American game.

Now, let's broaden the focus. 1963 was the centennial of the Emancipation Proclamation. By edict of Abraham Lincoln Negro-Americans were freed from slavery. Five years later, on July 28, 1868, the Fourteenth Amendment was added to the Constitution. In its opening paragraph it says:

All persons born or naturalized in the United States, and subject to the jurisdiction thereof, are citizens of the United States and of the State wherein they reside. No State shall make or enforce any law which shall abridge the privileges or immunities of citizens of the United States; nor shall any State deprive any person of life, liberty, or property, without due process of law, nor deny to any persons within its jurisdiction the equal protection of the laws.

That's clear, isn't it?

And so is the Fifteenth Amendment, which became law on March 30, 1870:

The right of citizens of the United States to vote shall not be denied or abridged by the United States or by any State on account of race, color, or previous condition of servitude.

These are the 1960s. The descendants of emancipated slaves are now demanding the rights which the Fourteenth and Fifteenth Amendments supposedly granted to our ancestors nearly a century ago.

Baseball is only a pastime, a sport, an entertainment, a way of blowing off steam. But it is also the national game, with an appeal to Americans of every race, color, creed, sex or political opinion. It unites Americans in the common cause of rooting for the home team.

Is it possible that Americans value victory for the home team more than the victory of democracy in our national life?

I ask this question in the light of two contrasting experiences. In 1962 I was awarded baseball's highest honor, membership in the Hall of Fame. I was welcomed to beautiful Cooperstown, New York, where high officials of baseball did everything in their power to make that day the happiest of my life. No one mentioned that I was the first Negro in the Hall of Fame, or that another bastion of prejudice had fallen.

No one was thinking about such things that day. I was thinking that the effort and energy I had put into playing ball for dear old Brooklyn had been recognized, that my name and record now stood beside those of Babe Ruth, Ty Cobb, Joe DiMaggio and the other guys who'd also played to win—if you'll pardon both the comparison and the cliché. And that small boys, some of them Negro boys, would visit Cooperstown in the future and read my plaque and say, "Did you ever see Jackie Robinson steal home, Dad? Show me how he did it when we go home, will ya, Dad?"

That fall James Meredith tried to enroll in the University of Mississippi. The Civil War, which had apparently ended in 1865, broke out anew. Soon the battlefront spread from state to state, from South to North. In my ball-playing days I had been invited to become a life member of the National Association for the Advancement of Colored People. The fee was $500 but I didn't know enough about the Association's aims to feel that I should contribute that sort of money to it.

But after I had retired from baseball I learned what the NAACP was doing to improve the lot of Negroes throughout the United States. I joined up and am now co-chairman of the life-membership recruiting drive. Now, suddenly, the NAACP and its allies are engaged in this new kind of war against prejudice, with as great a stake in freedom for our country as if we were being invaded by a foreign power.

I'd been in the first skirmishes of that democratic war, wearing a ball player's uniform. I was in it again, in 1963. With Floyd Patterson, Archie Moore, Curt Flood of the St. Louis Cardinals, and other Negroes of the sports and entertainment fields I went to Jackson, Mississippi, in January. We went there to stiffen the morale of those who were suffering economic and political oppression from the "Know-Nothings" of Mississippi.

Our stay in Jackson was brief and uneventful. We attended a banquet, made speeches and departed, inspired by the courage of those on the front lines, one of whom was the soon-to-be-martyred Medgar Evers.

In May the battle of Alabama began. Many warned me to avoid incurring the wrath of Bull Connor's police in Birmingham. Some people have asked why Floyd Patterson and I went there. We didn't have to go. We didn't go for what we personally might accomplish. The groundwork for resistance to Connor's rabid segregationists and the integration of Birmingham Negroes into the city's economic life had been laid by brave men and women under the leadership of Dr. Martin Luther King. Floyd and I went to Birmingham to give our thanks to the fighting people who were standing fast against fire-hoses, police dogs, riot clubs, guns and bombs.

Remember this: Cooperstown, New York, and Birmingham, Alabama, are both in the United States. In Cooperstown I had been a guest of honor in the company of three other new Hall of Famers: Bill McKechnie, Edd Roush and Bob Feller. In Birmingham I was "that negrah who pokes his nose into other peoples' puddin'."

From the moment of our arrival Floyd and I were watched like criminals come to town to plan a bank robbery, like potential despoilers of Southern womanhood.

We registered at the Gaston Motel in the Negro ghetto. We addressed a large assemblage in a Negro church. Our next destination was a second church where boys and girls waited to express their faith in the Birmingham fight for freedom. As we entered our car, state troopers blocked the driveway to prevent us from backing out. We waited until the police car moved away. As we started up the road, two other police cars came out of the night, forming a roadblock.

A young representative of the Southern Christian Leadership Conference was at the wheel. He hesitated. Would we be arrested for making a U-turn? He took the chance and sped away in the opposite direction.

As he parked before the second church, a young man approached.

"We saw what just happened," he said. "It won't happen here. There's strength in numbers. When you leave, fall in behind our cars and let them try to block us."

However, nothing out of the ordinary occurred and we drove back to the motel without incident.

The motel was a scene of destruction. It had been bombed a few days earlier. State and local police were massed outside, facing Negroes who were prepared to defend victims of fresh violence. Rumors were current that Klansmen were rallying in the city's outskirts.

The bomb had wrecked the dining room. Floyd and I had not eaten since our arrival in Birmingham, so we decided to look for a nearby restaurant. "There's one about two blocks away," we were told. "But you'd better be extremely careful. Don't speak to anyone on the street. The cops are hoping you'll start something, so they can pin a charge on you."

We looked neither to left nor to right as we walked the two blocks, a police car trailing us at the curb, parking before the little restaurant while we ate. Afterwards, it trailed us back to the motel.

The following morning Floyd and I paid our respects to the brother of Martin Luther King, the Reverend A. D. King, whose home had twice been bombed. The first bomb has been tossed on the lawn, twenty feet from the house. If it had hit its mark as the second bomb had, the dwelling would have been demolished, its occupants killed.

Among those we found in Rev. King's shattered home was a young man who said that he had been stopped by police while returning from work the previous evening. "Where's your identification?" an officer demanded. As he fished for his wallet, a second officer snarled, "Take that goddam cigarette outa your mouth, nigger!" Wallet or cigarette? Which order should he obey first? As he hesitated knuckles crashed into his face, bloodying his nose, knocking loose a tooth.

"Fighting back wouldn't have helped," he told us. "I'd be spending the next five years on a road gang. But in Birmingham Negroes are sick and tired of taking abuse. If it continues much longer we're going to fight back with their weapons."

"I saw five cops standing on a poor woman," another young man told me. "They picked her up, tossed her into a truck and took her off to jail. If they treat my sister like that I'll cut a cop's head off and fling it in the gutter!"

I don't know whether the young man's sister was one of the four innocent little girls who were slain by murderous bombers while learning the lesson of God's love in a Sunday-school class. That massacre revealed the depths to which the godless will go.

These horrors happened in the United States on the day Giants fans were cheering Willie Mays's two home runs and Dodger fans were shouting themselves hoarse after Tommy Davis's game-saving one-hand grab of a 400-foot wallop.

In Birmingham Negroes were saying, "If we gotta die we may as well take someone with us!" In ball parks whites were yelling, "We're with you, Willie! We're with you, Tommy! Attaboy!"

That's what this book is about . . . how integration has come to baseball and how it can be achieved in every corner of the land. And also what Negroes are really like and what we think about during these crucial days when we are standing up, demanding to be counted among the free.

2

July 4, 1906.

In no other profession has the color line been drawn more rigidly than in baseball. Colored players are not only barred from white clubs; at times exhibition games are cancelled for no other reason than objections raised by a southern player. These southerners are, as a rule, fine players and managers refuse to book colored teams rather than lose their services.

The colored player suffers great inconveniences while travelling. All hotels are generally filled from garret to cellar when they strike a town. It is a common occurrence for them to arrive in a city late at night and to walk around for several hours before finding a lodging.

The situation is far different today than it was in the 1870s, when colored players were accommodated in the best hotels in the country. The cause of this change is no doubt the sad condition of things from a racial standpoint today. The color question is uppermost in the minds of Americans at the present time.

The average pay of colored players is $466 a year, compared to an average of $2,000 for white major leaguers and $571 for white minor leaguers. The disparity in salaries is enormous when it is apparent that many colored stars would be playing in the majors but for the color line.

This picture was drawn by Sol White in 1906 in his *History of Colored Baseball*. With minor modifications it was true in 1945 when I was on the Kansas City Monarchs of the Negro National League.

Sol White was a hero of Negro baseball in the 1880s and 1890s, a .400 hitter on the original Cuban Giants and later manager of the invincible Philadelphia Giants. In the yellowed pages of his little book are valuable instructions in hitting and pitching, the histories of many fine teams of the times, as well as an exhortation to Negro youths to play hard, cleanly, and with respect for their opponents and the game.

According to White, baseball came late to Negroes. Bud Fowler was the first Negro to play on an otherwise white team, starring at second base for the New Castle champions of western Pennsylvania in 1872.

By 1880, twenty Negroes were on minor league rosters. I was not the first Negro in the major leagues. In 1884 Fleetwood Walker caught 41 games for the Toledo Mudhens of the big-league American Association, while his brother Weldon played the outfield in six games.

That June the Chicago White Stockings rolled into Toledo for an exhibition game. They were champions of the rival National League, a bruising crew of sluggers, four of whom batted over .340. Their manager and first baseman was Cap Anson, who would turn handsprings in his grave if he knew that I share a niche with him in baseball's Hall of Fame.

During his 27-year big-league career Anson played all nine positions. He batted over .300 in 22 seasons; his average was .394 in 1894, when he was forty-three years old. He was a great ball player but a heartless man.

In 1884 the nation was still recovering from the aftermath of the Civil War. Southern senators and congressmen were whipping up a fury of bigotry against Negroes in much the same vituperative language that many Southern demagogues use today. Whether Cap Anson was poisoned by their venom I do not know, but he walked on the field in Toledo that June day, saw the Walker brothers in uniform and stalked off, taking his team with him. A large crowd was in the stands. Charlie Morton, Toledo's manager, promised to fire the Walkers the next morning. The game was played.

Thereafter Anson saw red at the mere mention of a Negro in baseball. He launched a one-man crusade to rid the game of all but whites.

The following season John Montgomery Ward of the New York Giants watched George Stovy fan fifteen batters in an Eastern League game and recommended Stovy's purchase. When Anson heard about the pending deal his howls of rage could be heard from Chicago to New York. Negotiations were called off. Stovy spent the remainder of his career in segregated ball.

Anson's vendetta reached a climax in the winter of 1887-88. He appeared at major and minor league meetings, urging the adoption of a rule that would require owners to fire Negroes on their rosters and never again to contract with them. None was then in the majors; twenty-five in the minors were deprived of their jobs, among them Sol White and Weldon Walker.

Walker had played for Akron in the Tri-State League in 1887. He refused to take banishment lying down. His letter to President George McDermitt of the Tri-State League is a relic of one man's struggle for equality in that far off day:

> I have grievances, sir. I question whether my individual loss serves the public good. I write you not because I have been denied making my bread and butter, but in the hope that the league's action will be reversed. The rule that you have passed is a public disgrace! It casts derision on the laws of Ohio, the voice of the people, which says that all men are equal. There is now the same accommodation for colored and white men and women in your ball parks, and the same disposition is made of the moneys of both. I would suggest to your honorable body that if your rule is not repealed, you should make it criminal for black men and women to be admitted to your ball parks.

There should be some sounder cause for dismissal, such as lack of intelligence or misbehavior. Ability, intelligence, should be recognized first, last and at all times by everyone. I ask this question—why was this rule passed?

Weldy Walker received no reply.

John J. McGraw loved victory so passionately that he would have ordered his pitchers to dust off his grandmother if she'd been a .350 hitter with a home-run bat. As the third baseman of the rough and tough Baltimore Orioles of the 1890s he had been one of an invincible crew. But as their manager in the infant American League in 1901 he was in desperate need of players. That February he went to Hot Springs, Arkansas, to drown his worries in the thermal baths.

On a diamond near McGraw's hotel two Negro teams were playing. His eye was caught by the smart hitting and slick fielding of a copper-skinned second sacker, Charlie Grant. After the game, McGraw invited Grant to his suite.

Grant was a Negro, under contract to the Chicago Columbia Giants. He emerged from McGraw's suite a full-blooded Indian chief and an Oriole.

Newspapers reported Grant's signing. On March 5 a delegation of Chicago Negroes arrived in Hot Springs. As Baltimore baseball writers watched, they presented a floral tribute to their hero.

The following day McGraw received a telegram from National League President Nick Young, reminding him of the anti-Negro rule adopted at Cap Anson's instigation in 1888.

McGraw released Grant later that day.

In the long years between the late 1880s and the mid-1940s dark-skinned Americans played ball in a world of their own. Hundreds of independent Negro teams sprang up in the 1910s, some booking as many as 200 games a year. Leagues were formed, dissolved, and re-formed. During the sports-conscious 1920s, the Negro National League and Negro American League took firm root East and West. It was apartheid as in South Africa, except that occasionally a big league team, barnstorming after the season, met a Negro team and had a heck of a time holding its own. Negro ball was almost a carbon copy of the white game, with a regular schedule, an annual all-star game and World Series. As participants in these games will report later in these pages, attendance was high, often over 20,000 at World Series contests. Among those present were many enthusiastic white fans.

Negroes regarded their stars as the equals if not the superiors of many whites whose names they read daily in the box scores. In those days we had our own press, our theaters, churches and, of course, our segregated schools. Some progress toward integration in sports was taking place in the 1930s as Jesse Owens triumphed in the 1936 Olympics and during Joe Louis's dignified reign as heavyweight king. But organized baseball was closed to us.

Few of our diamond stars were known to white fans. Josh Gibson, the hammering home-run slugger, and Satchel Paige received occasional comment on white sport pages. Negro teams played in big and minor league parks, but white newspapers seldom reported their doings.

As for Negro fans—they longed to see the Homestead Grays or Kansas City Monarchs pitted against white world champions. How would Josh Gibson fare against Lefty Grove or Carl Hubbell? Could Satch stop Babe Ruth or Jimmy Foxx? No one will ever know.

Terris McDuffie was one of the many topnotch Negro hurlers of that period, a burly righthander with a busy baseball brain. Says Terris:

I'm Alabama-born and Florida-raised. Back in '29, when I was 18, I enlisted and they put me on the ball team at Fort Benning, Georgia. I was just a beginner. I played the outfield when I wasn't pitching for the regimental club, the 24th Infantry it was. The Colonel wanted winning sports teams, so he got officers to come down from West Point to coach us in special duties like baseball, basketball and track. Well, Satchel Paige and the Birmingham Black Barons—that's the team Willie Mays was on later—come over to play us. Satch must of liked what he saw of me. He told me he was going to keep his eye on me. The day he pitched at Fort Benning he threw so hard an average hitter couldn't get his bat around for a full swing. The only way to hit Satch was to choke the bat and half-swing—that's how quick he was! In all my years I never seen anyone who threw like him. Feller? No comparison! By the time Satch got on the Indians with Feller in '48 he'd lost his fast ball but he knew so much about pitching he could still make big-leaguers look silly.

When I finished my Army bit in '31 the Barons signed me. I pitched against Satch in '37 when he was with the Kansas City Monarchs and I was on the Newark Eagles. He shut me out, 6 to 0. That winter he fixed for me to go to Puerto Rico. I faced him on the Puerto Rico All-Stars . . . he was on an all-star colored team from the States. I beat 'em 4 to 0 with one hit. I lost two other games to Satch years later in Mexico. I concentrated on control. I had a sinker, a slider, a curve and different speeds and a good fast ball. My favorite pitch was my sliding sinker. I never had to use off-pitches like the knuckler or sneaky slow stuff. I started 27 games with the Eagles in '38 and finished 'em all without relief, 27 complete games in succession! I played the outfield days when I wasn't pitching. That year I was the most valuable player in the Negro National League. In '41 with the Homestead Grays I won 27 games and lost 5.

After the war I was getting the highest pay in the East, though not as high as Satch in the American League out West. I had a contract for $800 a month, with a $2,000 bonus at the end of the season, about $6,000 a year. That's not much compared to what the boys were getting in white ball, so when the Pasquel brothers offered me higher pay to jump to their Mexican League, I jumped along with Sal Maglie, Lou Klein, Max Lanier, Mickey Owen, Fred Martin and Danny Gardella. In

Mexico I played on mixed teams with players of big reputations in the majors for the first time. Well, as you know, the Mexican League didn't last long, and by 1950, when it broke up, the colored leagues in the States were busting up because the majors were taking their best players. I was forty or forty-one then, but I won the Most Valuable Player Award in Venezuela, pitching for Caracas in '51. The next year I went to Santo Domingo and won their MVP Award, too. Just before the '54 season the big push for colored stars was on in the States. I was forty-five but my arm was still good, so the Dallas Eagles of the Texas League sent for me. That was the only time I pitched for a mixed team. My stuff was as good as ever. I worked in 14 games, won three, lost four and held my earned run average down to 3.04. Then I badly injured my leg, could hardly walk on it for three or four years, and was finished. All told I played 24 years in professional ball.

Our home runs were not made off the jack-rabbit ball. Our hitters lambasted a ball inferior to the one used in the majors. We had no soreheads, swelled heads or braggarts. We trained in March like big-leaguers, but we didn't travel like them. If they'd traveled in cars and buses like we did, lost nights on the road trying to reach the next town, riding until game time the next day, eating the wrong food, how long do you think those highly touted stars would've lasted? We stood more wear and tear and hard knocks than them.

What's happening in baseball today is very impressive. I'm glad our boys are getting a chance to prove what they can do. They give fans what they want, they believe in themselves; they produce.

Bill Yancey is one of the few stars of Negro ball now employed in the big leagues. In the 1930s he was the all-star shortstop for the Philadelphia Giants, New York Lincoln Giants and the all but invincible Hilldales of Darby, Pennsylvania. Wintertimes he was the stonewall guard of the famous Renaissance Five which was recently admitted en masse to basketball's Hall of Fame. Today he is a scout for the New York Yankees, his most impressive protégé Al Downing, the strike-out prodigy.

*

I was born in Philadelphia and attended Central High from 1918 to 1922 but couldn't play on the basketball or baseball teams because I was a Negro. In fact, I never played on an organized team until after I was graduated.

The Philadelphia Giants tried me out in 1923, but I was too inexperienced to make the Negro big leagues then. They were owned by Bert Williams, who'd broken the Broadway color line with the Ziegfeld Follies. We had no Negro minor leagues to develop players in so I had to do my own developing where I could. I caught on with the Boston Giants as a shortstop. I didn't master that position until '28 when John Henry Lloyd, old Pop Lloyd—they've named a ball park for him in Atlantic City—taught me position play, showed me the right moves on the pivot, and how to work cut-offs and relays.

In 1929 I signed with the Lincoln Giants and was the first Negro player to put his foot on the grass at Yankee Stadium. We were scheduled to meet the Baltimore Black Sox in the first Negro game at the Stadium. I suited up early, ran out to right field and stood where the Babe stood and pretended to catch fly balls like him. Then I took a bat and went to the plate and pretended I was hitting one into the right-field seats like him. It was a bigger thrill than hitting my own first home run against the Paterson Silk Sox back in '24.

Thirty years ago Negro ball was at its peak. The Lincoln Giants often beat the Bushwicks when they were barnstorming with stars such as Lou Gehrig, Jimmy Foxx and others. White baseball writers didn't cover our league games although we often drew 10,000 to 15,000 fans and filled Comiskey Park in Chicago for our 1934 all-star game, which was run off as smoothly and was certainly as well played as the big-league show.

No one scouted me. No one scouted Josh Gibson. I've seen 'em all since the 1920s and Josh was the greatest right-hand hitter of all time, including Jimmy Foxx and Rogers Hornsby. Take Foxx—Josh could wrap him up! They say that Jimmy's homer to the last box in the third tier in left field at Yankee Stadium was the longest blow ever made there. I was playing in the Stadium against Josh's Homestead Grays when he lifted one two stories over the bullpen and out of the ball park! The Grays used Griffith Stadium in Washington while the Senators were on the road. That old park was the toughest in the majors on home-run hitters. But Josh hit eight homers in ten games in one span, more than all the Senator hitters in 77 games. Josh had great pride. Dizzy Dean often pitched postseason games against Negro teams Josh played on. One day the crowd was small and Diz was in a hurry to get away. He would never have done this in a regular game, but this was only an exhibition, so before the ninth inning he called to Josh: "Let's get the side out quick and get the heck out of here! Let three strikes go past you, will ya, Josh?" "Okay with me," grinned Josh. So Diz fogged one up to the plate. Josh swung. The ball went winging far over the fence. Josh laughed as he jogged around the bases. "That's more fun than taking three strikes!" he called to Diz.

Josh earned the top salary in the Negro leagues, $1,000 a month. He was still catching for the Homestead Grays in '47, the year Jackie Robinson became a Dodger. He was tickled to death the color line was broken, but he was a frustrated man, too old for the majors. Poor Josh let himself go. He got fat and quit in '48. Two years later he died.

✻

In 1936 Bill Yancey retired from active play, taking the job-hunting trail to Latin America.

I coached Colon in the Panama Isthmian League. Now, here's a funny one: Paul Richards was Colon's catcher, and as smart as he is today. But Colon hired me. Richards then went back to the States to manage the Atlanta Crackers, the White Sox, Orioles, and now he's general manager at Houston. I coached south of the border for seven and a half years, then came home to coach a Negro team. That's how the ball bounces!

Well, here I am, scouting for the Yankees and proud of Al Downing, a boy of the finest personal qualities who should star for the next ten or twelve years. He has no problems like Jackie or the others in the early days of integrated ball. Jackie went in tough and came out tough ten years later. He was lucky working for a man who liked the color of his hair. A boy's got to be tough in situations like Jackie's. Don't think I'm an angry old man. I'm doing all right. I've got work in the game I spent my young days in. I tell my wife we ought to get down on our knees every night—we're living beautifully compared to most Negroes.

3

I was born in 1919 on a plantation near Cairo, Georgia, a day's hike north of the Florida border. My parents were sharecroppers who lived on a white man's land. They gave the major part of their crops to him in lieu of cash for rent.

Like other Negroes of the Deep South my ancestors must have been slaves. Our family name, Robinson, no doubt was borrowed by us from a master. It is difficult to realize that one's great-grandparents were chattels without human rights, that they could be bought and sold with dollar values on their heads from birth to death.

By 1919 memories of the auction block, the whip, the chains that Abraham Lincoln was shocked to see shackled to Negroes' limbs, white men assaulting Negro virgins in the dark of night, backs broken by endless toil—all these memories were fading. Lynchings were fewer than in the early 1900s. The fiery cross of the Ku Klux Klan no longer intimidated us, but the habit of silence was still strong. It was even possible to point to some small steps toward recognition of our status as human beings. Booker T. Washington had been received in the White House in 1904 in acknowledgment of his work as an educator. George Washington Carver had won international acclaim as an agricultural chemist. In sports Jack Johnson had held the heavyweight boxing championship of the world.

During the 1920s of my boyhood our musicians traveled up the Mississippi from New Orleans to introduce jazz to the North; they were represented as the denizens of barrelhouses and brothels, and their syncopated rhythms as the throbbing of jungle drums. Our theatrical artists played before Negro audiences or, if to whites, in all-black troupes on sidestreet stages. Florence Mills, whose "Bye Bye Blackbird" was a No. 1 song hit in 1925, never sang it from the stage of a white vaudeville house.

The 1920s were called the Golden Age of Sports, but no Negro was permitted to face Jack Dempsey in the ring, Bill Tilden on the tennis courts, Bobby Jones on the links; no Negro pitcher faced Babe Ruth. No Negro could compete on equal terms with white business-men, professional men or skilled laborers. He entrusted his earnings to white bankers, he bought insurance from white agents—if he had money to bank or to buy insurance with. In many states he had no vote; where he enjoyed the franchise he was forced to choose between white candidates. He was a menial, a servant, an inferior, little freer than to move from place to place when and if he could afford it.

My mother is a religious woman. She had no formal education, but she possessed the wisdom to perceive that times were changing. And she was gifted with the courage to speak out in defense of her beliefs. She concluded that we could receive a superior education only in that part of the United States that was not corrupted by memories of the days when Negroes had been on a par with domestic animals.

To move away from the South required money, and to accumulate money was not easy. My parents labored from dawn to dark on the white man's land, then saw the products of their toil snatched from them. The plantation owner gave them a few dollars for the neces-saries of life, then took the dollars away by overpricing the goods they were forced to buy at his general store. Only by the greatest thrift could my mother save enough to buy the presents which she laid at the foot of our Christmas tree. She was always in our master's debt.

I was thirteen months old when my mother finally was able to buy train tickets to California for her children and herself. That this was possible at all was due to her insistence that my father demand a larger percentage in cash for his crops. She didn't have enough to buy a ticket for my father. He quit the plantation and took a job in Florida.

Our destination was Pasadena, where my mother's brother, Burton, worked as a gardener. Japanese were more acceptable as gardeners to the owners of great estates in Southern California. Uncle Burton hired himself out by the day, earning a fairly steady income by his self-taught skill as a landscape artist.

My mother refused to accept more from him than the roof over our heads. She went into the open labor market for work as a domestic. We children seldom saw her during the day; she was gone before we were up and did not return until we were in bed. She was hands caressing us or a voice in our sleep.

It was a treat when she brought us leftovers from her employers' dinner parties. I can remember days when we lived on sweet water and hard bread. We'd wait up, hoping she'd come home with a cake or pie. Most of those she worked for knew about our situation and let her fill her apron with whatever they didn't need. As for money, we seldom saw a dime.

Pasadena regarded us as intruders. My brothers and I were in many a fight that started with a racial slur on the very street we lived on. We saw movies from segregated balconies, swam in the municipal pool only on Tuesdays, and were permitted in the YMCA on only one night a week. Restaurant doors were slammed in our faces. In certain respects Pasadenans were less understanding than Southerners and even more openly hostile.

Such was my early childhood. I learned my lesson then. My mother taught us to respect ourselves and to demand respect from others.

That's why I refused to back down in later life and won't back down now.

I can't pinpoint the moment when I understood this, for my mother never put her philosophy into precise words. She couldn't write well, she made mistakes in grammar, but she expressed herself in a way that made me understand what she meant and how she felt. As I listened I acquired her ideas. Besides, I was aggressive by nature.

In kindergarten I had a teacher, Miss Haney, who judged me as an individual and not by the color of my skin. She inspired me to believe that my chances for equal treatment from others were as good as anyone else's, provided that I applied myself to the tasks at hand.

Then there was our minister, Reverend Karl Downs. We were devout Methodists. I don't profess to be the greatest churchgoer in the world. I believe a person can be quite religious and at the same time militant in the defense of his ideals. Like Reverend Downs, I believe in doing to others the things they have done unto me. I have practiced this principle all my life. Some of my friends tell me that I go overboard on this interpretation of the Golden Rule, that I do too much to others and get left out on a limb. Maybe so—no one is perfect.

Reverend Downs watched me play football on Saturdays and then made sure that I taught my Sunday-school class the following morning. He was a militant Christian who diplomatically induced others to do what he wanted them to do by his powers of persuasion. White Americans respected him, but when he was laid low by a critical illness a few years ago, he was wheeled to the Negro ward of a hospital instead of being rushed to the emergency room in the white wing. His death caused a public furor.

When I was about eight I discovered that in one sector of life in Southern California I was free to compete with whites on equal terms—in sports. I played soccer on my fourth-grade team against sixth-graders who were two or three years older than me. Soon I was competing in other sports against opponents of every size, shape . . . and color. We had plenty of space for team sports in Pasadena, and the weather was good around the calendar. The more I played the better I became—in softball, hard ball, football, basketball, tennis, table tennis, any kind of game with a ball. I played baseball against men's teams in my early teens. I played hard, and always to win.

Sports were the big breach in the wall of segregation about me. In primary and high school white boys treated me as an equal. I was their star, the leading scorer in basketball, quarterback in football, a

.400 hitter in baseball, the best broad-jumper on the track team. They made me a professional at eight by bringing me lunches as a bribe to play on their teams.

Many of my white teammates became, in the accepted sense, my friends. My brothers and I visited our next-door neighbors and the boys across the street, and they visited our home. I apparently enjoyed the normal social relations of a boy of high-school age.

I am using the term "social relations" in the usual sense, but there is a difference between "social" and "intimate" relations. Intimacy is possible only when a common basis of understanding exists. Friendship is a long and mutually selective process, possible only when two people have more in common than being around together from time to time.

Negroes and whites may meet socially, work together, live next door to each other, but true friendship is forged only when human beings are attracted to each other by common interests, common tastes, and the interplay of mutually acceptable ideas. It makes no sense to me to call a person a "friend" when no spark of recognition flashes between us, whether he is white or black. Today I live in a neighborhood in Stamford, Conn., which is otherwise white. My neighbors are friendly; there is no friction between us. But that does not mean that we are more than good neighbors.

My experiences in sports multiplied my contacts with whites. At an early age I met all sorts of people, traveled from place to place and saw life at firsthand.

I knew that the wall of segregation was not so high that it could not be breached on gridiron, court, diamond.

I put out in every game I played, winning four letters at Muir Technical High School, Pasadena Junior College, and UCLA. Football, baseball, basketball and track weren't enough to satisfy my desire to express myself fully in the only way open to me. I played tennis, golf, and always wanted to be top banana.

But in classroom work my will to excel wasn't there: I was a mediocre C. My brothers, their friends and acquaintances, all older than me, had studied hard and wound up as porters, elevator operators, taxi drivers, bellhops. I came to the conclusion that long hours over books were a waste of time. Considering my situation, I was not far wrong. My knowledge of life was increasing in sports and I was later to take a postgraduate course in the civil rights movement.

Those who argue that improved educational facilities for Negroes will solve the civil rights problem fail to understand that unless Negroes can use their education to the fullest extent in competition with whites, the crisis will continue unabated.

Of course, sports was far from a complete solution to my problems. Thousands might cheer as I raced to a touchdown, but many more thousands treated me as an invisible man from the moment I stepped through the clubhouse door and became Jackie Robinson, Negro.

Even while playing I was jolted by painful reminders of my status. In a Junior College basketball game a guard repeatedly roughed me to the accompaniment of nasty racial cracks. I was heading for a 30-point game when he dug his elbow into my belly. I gave him a jab in return.

"See you after the game," he warned.

"That's up to you," I replied.

He lunged at me as the final whistle blew. A ruckus started that soon became a full-sized riot in all parts of the gymnasium.

After peace was restored, the president of our opponent's student body visited our dressing room. He made an apologetic speech and asked me to shake hands with my opponent. "Certainly," I said.

But the bigot refused to soil his white hands on me. He created such a disturbance that his own teammates turned against him. Nevertheless, he would not shake my hand.

In a high-school football game I was brought down on the opening kickoff. My tackler gave me the knee as I tried to rise. He knocked the wind out of me, and, as I discovered later, broke two of my ribs. This occurred during my high-school days at Muir Tech. It was a bigot's reminder that he intended to drive me off the gridiron, singlehanded.

He did, for a while. The following year I was PJC's first string quarterback and field coach. On the squad were five Negroes, among them two regulars, Ray Bartlett and myself. And also six rugged white Southerners from Oklahoma. We had a superior team for junior college play, but our first few days with the fellows from Oklahoma were trying. It was as hard on them as it was on us. There was somewhat of a problem as far as attitude went.

Ray and I decided to expose the situation to Coach Tom Mallory. He said he couldn't understand our touchiness, that the three Negro substitutes hadn't complained, and that the Oklahomans had the greatest respect for Ray and me.

We told him we wanted more than respect; we wanted a winning team, twenty-five guys united to win. We said that if the Oklahomans persisted in their war of nerves we'd quit Pasadena and go to Compton Junior College, which was our fiercest rival.

Mallory paled. We had been attracting large crowds to home games in the Rose Bowl. The specter of Compton walking all over Pasadena frightened him.

I don't know what Mallory said to the Oklahomans, but their attitude changed and the team suddenly jelled. We ran up a 16-game winning streak and were hailed as the best junior college team in the country. As the next season drew to a close and our graduation approached, the Oklahomans passed the word around that all of us, Negro and white, should enter a big-time university as a unit, and go on to national football honors.

I declined their proposition, although not because they made it. I was receiving all sorts of offers for football scholarships. A central California college promised me an apartment for my mother and myself, and accommodations for my girl friend, if any. They offered me a monthly allowance plus a lump sum to be deposited in a bank until I graduated. But I decided to enter UCLA because it was nearer home and my mother, who had worked hard throughout the Depression to put me and my brothers through school.

At UCLA I gained plenty of publicity on sports pages. I won high scoring basketball honors in the Pacific Conference two years in a row. In 1940's final game UCLA was rated well below Southern California. My closest scoring rival was a USC forward. "Don't worry about him, Jackie," said the white UCLA guard assigned to cover him. "I'll take care of this guy good and plenty tonight."

We lost the game, but my teammate lived up to his promise and I won the scoring race.

I received this kind of co-operation from white teammates because in my turn I subordinated personal ambitions to team play. The following year we were in a very close game and I was locked in a battle for the scoring title. A freeze was on. The ball came to me. I had an easy set shot before me. I passed the ball, maintaining the freeze. To have broken the pattern would have been a betrayal of my teammates' confidence in me. Winning the game meant more than the possible loss of the scoring title.

A baseball career was far from mind in 1941. Organized ball was a white man's game. Negro professionals played in the distant East and barnstormed through the South, so I never saw them in action. I vaguely thought of becoming a football or basketball coach in some Negro college.

But I was playing baseball in school and out. I won all-league honors as shortstop of the Pasadena Sox of the Southern California Amateur League over Vern Stephens, who was to star later on the St. Louis Browns and Boston Red Sox.

We called ourselves the Sox because the Chicago White Sox met us in a postseason exhibition game which was really designed to raise money for our athletic equipment.

I recall having a good day against the White Sox—two or three hits and a couple of steals. Afterward, I heard that Jimmy Dykes, who was managing the Sox then, said that if I were white he could get $50,000 for me.

I swallowed hard when I heard that story. In those prewar days, $50,000 was a lot of money.

In 1938 Colonel Leland Stanford MacPhail became president of the Brooklyn Dodgers. MacPhail was a skilled baseball operator with a brainful of highly original notions. He had lifted the virtually bankrupt Cincinnati Reds out of the National League cellar before moving on to Ebbets Field. By 1940 he had shrewdly traded the indigent Dodgers into contenders in the National League pennant race. They won the flag in '41.

I rooted for the underdog Dodgers in that year's World Series with the Yankees. I suffered agonies when Mickey Owen missed Hugh Casey's third strike with two out in the ninth inning of the fourth game. The Dodgers were leading 4-3, when Tommy Henrich raced to first base. Yankee batters staged a 4-run rally to win, 7-4, and went on to win the Series.

What a Series. . . .

Then, two months later . . . Pearl Harbor!

Every American, Negro or white, rallied to defend our country. If Negroes found themselves segregated in the armed services, this was no different from our condition before war was declared. I was drafted and sent to Fort Riley, Kansas, assigned to a Special Services battalion in the cavalry, which meant mobile units such as tanks then.

I was too busy at Fort Riley in 1942 to keep up with the big-league races. Things were happening far away in Brooklyn that were to change the course of my life soon after the war ended. MacPhail's Dodgers won 104 games yet lost the pennant to the St. Louis Cardinals. He resigned to enter the Army at the season's end. He was succeeded by Branch Rickey, long the highly successful Cardinal general manager and the most fearlessly independent magnate in the game.

Early in '43 I was commissioned as a lieutenant and assigned to Camp Hood, near Waco, Texas, where I was in command of an all-Negro tank battalion. The spirit of the men was high and my CO suggested that I go overseas as a morale officer with Negro troops. I might have gone but for an incident which indicated that Texas was, in some respects, as hostile to Negro-Americans as Germany or Japan.

One evening I boarded a bus at the Officers' Club with another lieutenant's wife. She was light-skinned; I am dark. We took seats in the middle of the bus as it began the trip through the camp to the gate, where I planned to transfer to another bus for Waco.

We had gone but a short distance when the civilian driver braked to a stop and strode down the aisle. "Get going, now!" he snapped. "Get to the rear!"

"I'm not going anywhere," I retorted. "I'm staying here."

He turned tail, returned to his post, started the bus, eyeing me through the rear-view mirror. The sight of a Negro sitting beside a woman who might well be white seemed to infuriate him. At the next stop he shouted: "Hey, you! Get back to the rear! There'll be trouble at the gate if—"

"There's no segregation on post buses," I rejoined. "That's official regulations."

He jumped up and headed for me. I rose to meet him. Epithets spewed from his lips. I leveled my finger at him and told him off. He retreated, put the bus in gear and stomped on the gas.

At the gate he leaped out, ran to the dispatcher. As my companion and I got off I heard him say, "That's the one, that's the nigger who's been givin' me a hard time!"

"I'm not looking for trouble," I said. "But for your own good, you better leave us alone."

A loud argument began. At that moment a jeep drove up. An MP approached. "Sir," he said, addressing me, "are you having trouble here?" The driver bleated that he intended to file charges against me, a Negro who had dared disobey a white man. The embarrassed MP suggested that we settle the dispute at the provost marshal's office. "Glad to do it," I said.

But in the provost marshal's office I was convinced that it was Southern tradition versus Negro. I was charged with drunkenness, although I have never taken an alcoholic drink in my life. I was charged with conduct unbecoming an officer and a gentleman. I was charged with willful disobedience and disrespect.

I faced court-martial and dishonorable discharge.

I refused to fight the charges in the press, but my fellow officers did. They sent letters to the NAACP, the Pittsburgh Courier and the Chicago Defender. The NAACP demanded an inquiry. The newspapers asked for details. Before I knew what was happening the upper echelons of Camp Hood were being bombarded with protests.

The charges were reduced in number and I was exonerated at a formal hearing. It was a small victory, for I had learned that I was in two wars, one against the foreign enemy, the other against prejudice at home.

Meantime, my chance of going overseas vanished. I was transferred from camp to camp as an athletic director of Negro recruits. Late in '44 1 was separated from service and picked up a few dollars playing football on the Los Angeles Bulldogs. That winter I coached a Negro college basketball team in Austin.

Coaching seemed small potatoes compared to morale-building in the ETO. While the Big Push was on into Germany that spring I signed with the Kansas City Monarchs for $400 a month.

The future looked dim. The staggering schedule in the Negro league, the long bus trips, low pay and, above all, the humiliating segregation might have depressed me if I hadn't played hard, driven myself hard in order to forget the indignities I'd suffered in Camp Hood.

Then, by a peculiar sequence of events the barred door to organized baseball opened just enough to give me hope. Wendell Smith, sports writer for the Pittsburgh Courier, covered the Negro league games. Smith had learned that a Boston Councilman was threatening to fight to repeal the ordinance permitting Sunday ball unless the Red Sox opened the door to Negro players. I do not know the politics behind Councilman Mutchnik's move, but it enabled Smith to arrange a tryout for Marvin Williams, Sam Jethroe and me at Fenway Park.

We worked out; we staged a thoroughly professional show, we were told we would be notified if we were wanted.

The following day President Roosevelt died. We never heard from the Sox.

That summer Clyde Sukeforth, the Brooklyn scout, came to Chicago, where the Monarchs were playing, and asked me whether I would go to New York to see Branch Rickey. He did not know why Mr. Rickey wanted to see me. I had heard he was attempting to organize a third Negro league with a Brooklyn entry in it.

"Okay," I told Sukey. "I'll go."

There came that unforgettable day when I first entered the Dodgers' office on Brooklyn's Montague Street and faced Branch Rickey.

He was like no one I had ever met. He seemed to know more about the problems that Negroes face than any which man in my experience. He knew every taunt, dig, threat, and underhand device of the bigots. He shouted their damnable curses at me, then pulled up sharply. "Can you take it?" he demanded. "Can you take it without fighting back?"

I didn't think I could. I didn't see why I should.

"If you can," he continued, "I'll sign you to a contract with our Montreal club. And if you play the kind of ball you're capable of, I'll put you on the Dodgers when you're ready, physically and mentally, to break this thing wide open!"

"I—I think I can."

"Thinking isn't enough. Can you?"

"I can."

$\mathcal{P}$rofessional sports is hardly the place to look for men with ideals, yet among the many who devote their lives to it are sincere and even dedicated idealists. Branch Rickey is baseball's most farsighted innovator; he has never lost sight of the old-fashioned virtues while directing the affairs of successful ball clubs. His respect for the opinions and rights of others, including Negroes, roused the enmity of lesser men. Both in St. Louis and Brooklyn his motives were impugned; he was ridiculed, his character was attacked. Happily, he has survived the puny darts of his adversaries.

He was sixty-four in 1946 when I first met him. Seventeen years later, at a time when integration had become the dominant issue in American social and political life, when bombs, bullets and mass arrests were the segregationists' barbaric retort to Negroes' demands, he sat in a New York hotel room, white-browed, cane across his knees, and recalled his preparations for my induction into baseball:

In 1943 the Brooklyn Trust Company, represented by George V. McLaughlin, was the Dodgers' angel. We had just $900,000 in the bank. I assumed then and so did George V. and Jim Mulvey—the two interests, the bank's and the Ebbets-McKeever group, which split control of the club—that we had to find fresh material. But those who say that I tried to find a suitable Negro player because of the wartime shortage of players are wrong.

I laid the cards on the table that first week in Brooklyn. In St. Louis I had had no way of dealing with the problem of bringing

Negro players into baseball. Why not? Because the Negro was not even allowed to pay his way into the grandstand at Sportsman's Park. That was the situation in St. Louis. I did everything I could, but I couldn't do a thing.

I made up my mind that the first thing I'd do, no matter where I went after St. Louis—it would have been the same if I'd gone to any other town than Brooklyn—the first thing I was going to do was to look into the Negro situation. McLaughlin was for it; he was sympathetic completely.

I said, "I have about half a dozen problems to face first."

He said, "What are they?"

I told him. I said, "The first thing is ownership—I don't own a dime's worth of stock. I must have the approval of ownership."

He said, "We will call a meeting."

He notified Joe Gilladeau, Jim Mulvey and George Barnwell, the other directors. We went to the Athletic Club for lunch, and George V. took charge. He made a speech before we adjourned at two-thirty. "My God, Rickey, you've got to know you're doing this not to solve any great sociological problem!" George V. said. "That's not it, now! You've got to have a ball player. I want to know your purpose."

I said, "First, to win a pennant. I think there's some good colored players. The second reason is . . . it's right!" Then I went into what they call the "race question." They were not opposed to my position on the race question at all! They were for it!

I had heard there was a rule in the National League forbidding the signing of colored players. I investigated. I could not find such a rule in any league or book. Cap Anson may have tried to get such a rule passed in 1888, but if it was ever adopted it was never recorded in any league minutes.

At a joint meeting of the major leagues in 1945 I announced my intention of signing a Negro. You won't get the owners to discuss that meeting. Some weren't there—they sent their general managers or some other representative. Fifteen clubs were represented. Fourteen of 'em adopted a resolution opposing Negroes in big-league ball—I abstained. It was a warning to me, an admonition strongly worded. It was read to me by one of the club presidents. He was violently opposed. He warned that the physical properties of the ball clubs, the parks, would go up in smoke. "That'll be the end of you!" I was told. "You'll get evasion. . . ."

Where is that document? Where has it gone? Someone picked up the paper after the meeting. If you ask about it, they'll lie!

I had never let any magnate know that I was scouting for a Negro. I never tried to find an ally among them. I disguised my intentions. I pretended I was scouting for Negro players for a mythical team to be called the Brown Dodgers. I spent $30,000 of Brooklyn money, and lost it all. We organized that racket colored league—that's what it was, pure racket. My scouts didn't know I was looking for a Negro for the Dodgers. Wid Mathews, who worked beside me, comes from the Deep South. In my opinion he was opposed to Negroes in big-league ball, but all for their playing in a Negro league. He did the first scouting for me. It was Wendell Smith, who wrote for a colored newspaper, who brought Robinson to my attention. I sent George Sisler out to scout him, and he thought he was doing it for the Brown Dodgers, too. Then Clyde Sukeforth took over as my close personal representative to handle negotiations with Robinson. He could have been suspicious because of my tremendous interest. But he wasn't—that is, until the second time I sent him to Robinson with instructions to bring the boy to Brooklyn to see me, and to find out all sorts of details such as where Robinson could play best. I think that Clyde suspected it then.

And when Robinson came, and I had that day with him, telling him about all the pitfalls and horrors he must expect, no one, no one in the whole wide world knew why he was there.

So I put on a Montreal uniform that '46 spring and began the slow and painful struggle to play the best ball I could while ignoring the vilification which greeted me almost daily. During spring training my manager, Clay Hopper, sat in the stands with Mr. Rickey watching me work out.

"Mr. Rickey," said this soft-voiced and gentle Mississippian, "you don't mean to say, do you, that Negrahs are human beings?"

Mr. Rickey's choice of Montreal as the setting for my home games could not have been improved. Canadians regarded me as a United States citizen who happened to have a colored skin. Some of my fellow Americans, especially in Baltimore, regarded me as an obscenity, a savage little above the level of a jungle beast, and told me so in vile language. I regarded myself as a lucky fellow, lucky to have been given the chance to play for good pay; for my ideas about civil rights were not as yet formulated. I played as I had always played, hard. I won the batting championship and led the International League in runs scored and in fielding averages for second baseman.

As I was saying good-bye to my teammates in September, Clay Hopper called me aside. "Jackie," he said, "I'd sure like to have you back on the Royals next spring. I hope Mr. Rickey won't call you up."

I was still in a Montreal uniform as spring training began in '47. Mr. Rickey had booked Dodger-Royal exhibition games in Panama in order to avoid clashes with segregationists in Florida. Rumors spread that I would become a Dodger on the season's opening day.

On the Dodgers were half a dozen Southerners as well as a few Northerners with minds prejudiced against Negroes. Led by Dixie Walker, they decided to file a petition with Mr. Rickey protesting against my coming.

Says Mr. Rickey:

The ones that protested against Robinson in Panama, I met them one by one and interviewed them in my room in a different hotel from theirs. Bob Bragan was one of them. What he said then made him a potential manager in my mind because of his complete forthrightness and complete honesty. When I asked him if he was opposed to Robinson he said,

"Yes, sir!"

"You're against him?"

"Yes, sir!"

"Will he affect your playing?"

"No, sir!"

Bragan opposed Robinson, but he was resolved to give me all the baseball he had in him.

Dixie Walker had left Panama because of an illness in his family. He wrote me a letter, asking me to trade him if Robinson became a Dodger. Later he came to me in person and said, "It's all right for you to trade me, sir, but not for the reason I gave you in my letter." Walker had been with the Dodgers for a long time. I got to know him much better through his actions during the year and a half when he was a teammate of Robinson's. My sympathies for him were aroused by what he did when Robinson took that terrible tirade from Ben Chapman, who was managing the Philadelphia club then. Robinson stood there without flinching—he nearly turned white doing it.

Robinson was taking it out there on the diamond and Dixie Walker challenged Chapman. "You wouldn't say these things to him off this field," Walker said. "You're a coward!" Eddie Stanky, who came from Alabama, backed Walker up. And so did the rest of the Dodgers. Harold Reese, who comes from Kentucky, had his picture taken with his hand on Robinson's shoulder. That was a very helpful thing, too.

Dixie Walker has a good mind. In my book he is a high-class gentleman, a quiet inside assimilator. He was bold enough, strong enough to write me that longhand letter asking me to trade him, that he couldn't play on a team with a colored fellow, and then to come to me and ask me to give him the letter back. He didn't want to be traded because he didn't want to hurt the club.

Integration in baseball started public integration on trains, in Pullmans, in dining cars, in restaurants in the South long before the issue of public accommodations became daily news. It started that spring wherever twenty-five boys sat down to eat with a colored man among them. It created an impossible situation for Southerners who didn't want them to eat together. Integration started on the blind side, which is where it should start if you want to solve the problem without violence or legislation, whites and Negroes acting together under natural circumstances, in natural surroundings.

The most ticklish problem in hiring a Negro was acceptance by the player's colleagues. That couldn't be done until he actually joined them. After the meeting in Panama I played Robinson all the time. He was going great. I was playing him so objectors would say, "This old virgin intends to bring him on our team." I didn't want the fuss in Panama to get in the papers. Keeping it out of the press was very gratifying to me. The players were not too proud of their stand. There's no doubt about Pee Wee Reese being a humanitarian who recognizes the rights of other people. He was one of the earliest to give Robinson quiet support and encouragement, lockerwise and otherwise. He was a great help in that time of trouble. But some Northerners on the team were red-necks and goddammers against Robinson.

As for other magnates, they took a position against me privately. They were moved by economic motives in '47, and again later, when they themselves hired Negroes.

Those who believe that the unreconstructed rebels of the South can never be brought to accept the Fourteenth and Fifteenth Amendments may learn the contrary from Dixie Walker. Soon after the '47 season began, Dixie's innate fairness and love of baseball made him cross the color line and come to me. I was lying on the trainer's table in Boston while Doc Wendler was giving me a rub-down. Dixie poked his head through the door. Now, Dixie was one of the most scientific hitters of all time. His level swing and wrist action enabled him to place a ball almost anywhere he wanted to. That morning he started to talk to me. In his soft Southern voice he gave me a lecture on how to hit behind runners, how to avoid hitting into double plays, how to shift my feet with a runner on third so that a fly ball would enable him to score standing up. And much more as he talked on, adding percentage points to my future batting average and RBI figures.

Now, many years later, Dixie is the Milwaukee Braves' batting coach. He was asked recently to explain how his ideas about Negroes had been affected by integration in baseball. He agreed, then changed his mind because "I want to forget what happened then."

But he went on to say that he had devoted many hours to coaching such Negroes on the '63 Braves as Lee Maye and Mack Jones. "Jones has great potential as a hitter," Dixie drawled. "He has power to all fields. And tremendous speed. He murdered the ball in batting practice this season. But in a game he still leaned forward with his body ahead of his bat, and lost power. But I have great hopes for this boy. He has everything in his favor. We sent him down to the minors in midseason so he could play every day. I'm going to try to make him into another Henry Aaron."

Dixie credits Negroes with maintaining the high level of big-league play during recent years when minor league farm systems have been reduced almost to the vanishing point. "They've made many contributions to the game," he says. "I don't know if anyone has said it yet, but I'm going to say it here—without the Negro we'd be unable to field clubs of major league quality in this expansion period."

In 1949, two years after Bobby Bragan's forthrightness had won Mr. Rickey's admiration, he was appointed manager of the Dodger farm club in Fort Worth. He won a Texas league pennant that year and has managed almost continuously since then in the high minors and majors, with terms in Pittsburgh and Cleveland before becoming Milwaukee's pilot in 1963.

With typical frankness he tells how integration in baseball has freed him from the prejudices that led him to sign the petition against me in 1947:

I was born in Birmingham but I wouldn't say that I had the same ideas as some others born down South. At the time Jackie joined the Dodgers, I am sure that I wouldn't have invited him to sit with me in the dining car—or in the same hotel room—whereas Ralph Branca and some of the boys born up North would. Jackie was a real gentleman. Jackie wouldn't sit with any white player that first year unless he was asked to. But before the season was over I was often in the same group with him at tables in dining cars, hotel rooms and, later, in card games. I think it's just a matter of becoming acclimated to the thing by association. I was exposed to integration daily under the shower, in the dressing room, in the next locker, on the bus, in the hotel and in many conversations. The exposure of my seven brothers and two sisters in the South has been limited. They can't feel the same tolerance that I feel today.

But even with them there are differences. My youngest brother Frank is married to a Puerto Rican girl and is living in Puerto Rico at the present time and very happily. They have three little daughters. The brother next to him, Jimmy, played professional ball and is now a scout for the Cincinnati Reds—he has been thrown together with Negroes; he ate with 'em, dressed with 'em, played ball beside 'em— he has the same acceptance that I do. But the other members of the family who have never been out of Birmingham, so to speak, still are intolerant. It's merely a matter of education.

I can cite changes in me from a personal standpoint. I have been in Jackie's home up in Connecticut. Howard Cosell, the sports broadcaster, is a personal friend of mine. Howard lives fairly close to Jackie, and often visits him. Jackie and I meet now on a purely social basis.

Dixie Walker and I, along with Whitlow Wyatt and Jo-Jo White, have spent hours coaching Mack Jones. It doesn't make any difference to us that Mack is a Negro. We're primarily concerned with making

Mack into another Henry Aaron. I am sure that Dixie, Whitlow and Jo-Jo—they're all from the South, too—feel the same as I do.

When I was with the Dodgers as a coach in 1960, my boy Bobby junior, who goes to Mississippi State College, was on the Dodger Junior Team in California. One of the members of his team was Kenny Washington's boy. Bobby junior used to bring Kenny junior out to our house or let him off at his own apartment. He'd think nothing of Kenny riding with him or riding in Kenny's car; whereas when I was seventeen or eighteen that would have been the furthest thing from my mind. And yet my wife and I think nothing of it now.

And just last week Mrs. Bragan was on a television show in Milwaukee with Lee Maye, the Braves' outfielder, which would have been very difficult for her to do twenty years ago.

My association with Maury Wills when I managed out in Spokane is one of my finest memories of this game. One of the finest contributions I have made to baseball was trying to mold Maury into a major-leaguer. I say this not to be immodest but because it's one of the finest bits of satisfaction I've derived from baseball, having a small part in Maury's success. I've had under my wing Roman Mejias, Roberto Clemente, Lino Dinoso, the two Aaron boys, Henry and Tommy, and many others. I managed many Negroes during my four yeas down in Cuba. Our two youngsters, Mrs. Bragan and I were thrown into this integration situation down there as well as up here. My two children attended integrated schools in Havana.

All of this adds up to a tolerant attitude, a little more understanding of the situation than if we'd never left Alabama.

> I've thought about this in relation to the happenings in Birmingham in recent times. My home now is in Fort Worth, where they integrated the schools last fall. Coming from Birmingham where they've had these ugly things happen on the level of school integration I believe the situation in Birmingham was not handled correctly.

Intolerance is not limited to Birmingham . . . it's to be found in Mississippi, Louisiana, Florida and in northern states, I don't know how long it's going to take to create a feeling of acceptance on the part of everybody. Like I say, it's a matter of exposure. To try to stop integration, to actively resent it, is a mistake. Any group that wants to demonstrate for its rights is entitled to be heard. It's wrong to make an issue of desegregation. That's my feeling. As for Old Miss and the Meredith case, my son goes to Mississippi State, two of my brothers graduated from there. My son tells me that the highways in Mississippi are the worst in the nation because they don't want to take federal funds down there so they can run their affairs as they please. I'm not a politician. I've got nothing to gain from criticizing Mississippi, but it looks to me like Mississippi is cutting off its nose to spite its white face. Baseball has handled the integration question the right way. Baseball has accepted Negroes. No resentment stems from Southerners in baseball any more. When a Negro puts a run up on the scoreboard no one questions the color of the run.

And I'll say this about 1947—sure, there were five or six of us resented Robinson's joining the team. But by that fall, when the Series checks were being passed out, Dixie Walker and Ed Head and all of us who were there, we had our hands out just as big as the next one—and Jackie Robinson had had the biggest hand of all in getting us into the World Series.

✷

Branch Rickey
Photo courtesy of National Baseball Hall of Fame Library, Cooperstown, NY.

$\mathcal{T}$he cards seemed stacked against Mr. Rickey during that spring of 1947. He had suppressed the Panama rebellion, but his program for my peaceful integration was complicated by Leo Durocher's suspension on the day of our arrival in Brooklyn from the South. Lurid headlines greeted my debut; threats of strikes against me by the Cardinals, Cubs and Phillies loomed over the horizon.

A glimpse into the behind-the-scenes maneuvers of those days is offered by Bill Yancey:

In '47 I heard that the Phillies were giving Robinson the hardest time of any team in the National League. It was common talk around Philadelphia that Ben Chapman was trying to provoke him into doing something that would get him driven out of the league.

The following fall I asked a Philly coach what was behind it all. He said Chapman had held a clubhouse meeting that spring and ordered his players to call Jackie every dirty name in the book. He also hired a coach to sit on the bench and yell thises and thats at him every time he went to bat.

The yelling and cursing seemed to have no effect on Jackie, he said. The Dodgers were in first place in August or September, and the Phillies were last. Chapman called another meeting and told him to lay off Jackie.

"Don't get him madder than he is," he said.

Bench-jockeying is usually for laughs in baseball. It was for keeps during the first years of integration on the diamond. The deliberate baiters were trying to provoke us into acts that would reflect on our character. They failed, just as other bigots have failed more recently wherever mass arrests and violence have been employed in the hope of provoking riots and bloodshed. When Mr. Rickey told me to turn the other cheek he was preaching nonviolence as it is being preached by Negro leaders in today's great struggle for total integration everywhere.

The baiter's vocabulary is limited only by the degree of his hatred for minority groups. He talks gutter language, using terms which are intended to demean. The newly arrived immigrant is called *mick, dago, kike, spick,* until he is assimilated into the majority of white native-born Americans. It is into this majority that the Negro, born here of ancestors who were brought here in chains centuries ago, can never be assimilated until the true meaning of democracy, of equality, is understood by all.

Oddly enough, some fair-minded whites are more sensitive to certain chauvinistic expressions than we are. A white playwright recently read me his latest work. In the dialogue the word *nigger* appeared in the mouths of several anti-Negro characters. Later, while we were discussing his play he used the word *nigger,* turned scarlet and stammered an apology.

I told him that I knew he was without prejudice, that his play was intended to help the Negro cause, that *nigger* appeared in it quite correctly, and that I was not in the least offended by his inadvertent repetition of the word. The words that offend us, I said, are those which are used with intent to disparage.

Nigger is offensive only when employed in a derogatory sense. The dictionary notes that it is "sometimes used as an expression of contempt." Some Negroes use it as a friendly form of address, quite as anyone might say, "How are you, you old son of a bitch?"

We object to *boy* or *girl* in reference to adult Negroes. My ire flares when anyone addresses me as "boy," even without intent to belittle. *Girl*, as applied to a woman who is a mother or even grandmother, is particularly insulting. Some progress has been made in eliminating these hangovers of slavery, but not enough.

Millions of words were published about me during my Dodger days. Heavyweight thinkers pondered over me as a forerunner of general desegregation in American life. Lightweights discussed me as if I were a creature from outer space, not quite human.

Dodger writers gave generous space to my play, and were scrupulously fair. However, they fell into the habit of calling me "the Dodgers' *Negro* star" in their accounts of games. This was like calling Carl Furillo "Italian" or Gene Hermanski "Polish." Several years were to pass before copy editors blue-penciled *Negro* into limbo. *Negro* in newspaper stories should be used only as a means of identification, like "blue-eyed" or "red-haired."

Negro newspapermen had never sat in baseball press boxes until I became a Dodger. Dodger writers eyed Wendell Smith uneasily as he watched games from the coop in Ebbets Field. His presence hampered the free expression of certain writers' opinions about me.

During that 1947 spring a New York afternoon paper reporter broke into a heated discussion with: "Yeh, Robinson may be going good now, but I tell you, colored boys have no endurance. He won't last the season out." This was typical of the slanders that Negroes stink, abuse their bodies with dissipation, and are inherently lazy.

Then there was the veteran morning paper writer who croaked: "Rickey's nuts! He'll ruin the game! Those dinge fans of Robinson's'll tear down the ball park if an umpire dares to put him out of a game! And there'll be a race riot the first time he steals second, spikes high, on a Southern infielder!"

The voice of a Pittsburgh writer came floating down to me as I darted down the third-base path, trying to unsettle a Pirate pitcher. "Showboat!" he screeched. "Looka the showboat!"

As time went on I became personally acquainted with writers throughout the circuit in interviews before and after each game. On road trips I had private talks with several whom I trusted. I made mistakes.

For example, I spoke quite openly about my problems with Milt Gross, sports columnist of the *New York Post,* whose name I mention here only as typical of the newsman who plies his trade under the cloak of assumed friendship when he is really lying in wait for an inside story. Gross had a way of offering me friendly advice. I made remarks which he subsequently used out of context, and with comment which, I felt, distorted my point of view.

I do not blame Gross, who was intent on doing his job well. Negroes in the public eye must be extraordinarily cautious when speaking for direct quotation, especially on the subject nearest their hearts, the improvement of their relations with whites. Interviewers who have had small experience in this field consciously or unconsciously mislead their readers by coloring their stories with their private opinions.

An example of this recently appeared in a column by John Drebinger in the *New York Times.* Drebbie is a veteran sportswriter with a reputation for accuracy. His column was apparently a sympathetic attempt to portray the progress of integration in baseball. He recalled a $25-a-plate banquet given a few years ago by the Variety Club of Dallas in honor of Eddie Brannick, the Giants' road secretary.

The banquet occurred during a joint exhibition tour by the Giants and Cleveland Indians. As the speechmaking began, 15 seats reserved on the dais for Negro players were vacant. They had apparently decided that they would not enter the hotel as the Variety Club's guests after having been barred from staying at it by the management.

Then, before the oratory ended, Willie Mays arrived and jokingly told the diners that he had been delayed by four flat tires. His ad-lib talk was the hit of the evening.

I wasn't there. I don't remember being asked by Drebbie for my opinion about Willie's belated appearance, but since he says so, it must be true. Perhaps he interviewed me by telephone.

In his column he quoted me as criticizing Willie's breaking of the players' boycott against the hotel. According to him I said, "Baseball was making great progress in the South then, and he should not have done anything to set it back."

I never said it. I could not have said it. I believe that Negroes should seize any and every opportunity to pierce the wall of segregation wherever it has been erected: South, North, East or West. Those Negro players who stayed away were entitled to make their own decision. In my opinion they decided wrongly.

Willie did right.

Deliberate distortions are common in the publications with avowed segregationist views. But when a national weekly publishes an article which flagrantly misrepresents the attitude of Negroes toward their white teammates, the effect is deplorable.

A few years ago a writer for a sports periodical asked me to verify a report that Negro big-leaguers were banded together against white players. Wasn't it true that they used a secret language of their own, ridiculing whites before their faces? Wasn't it true that George Crowe, then with Cincinnati, was their leader?

I denied the existence of such a cabal, such a code language or that George Crowe could have organized a Negro clique. Crowe was the most articulate and far-sighted Negro then in the majors. Younger Negroes turned to him for advice, I said, but only on a personal basis. As for a secret language . . . that was ridiculous. Like any other group of common origin, Negroes use certain words derived from common experience, just as Italians, Jews and Irish do. Such an article would be based on the wishful thinking of prejudiced minds.

Crowe also denied the truth of the report when the writer approached him.

Nevertheless, the article was circulated nationally with the fabricated quotes. It was a mischievous piece of propaganda.

Bigots descended to the vicious baiting of my wife while she watched me play in Baltimore during my International League days. They tried to unnerve me with threats against my life. Later, in Brooklyn, I received a letter warning me I would be shot from the stands if I dared play in a doubleheader against the Reds in Crosley Field. I handed it to a club representative.

My teammates gave me a good old-fashioned ribbing on the bus to the ball park. When we went on field we saw police scattered through the stands and learned that FBI agents were at the gate, scanning faces for cranks and crackpots.

"Let's all wear Number 42 on our backs," quipped Gene Hermanski. "Okay with me," I retorted. "And paint your faces black and run pigeon-toed."

No one shot at me, of course, but, after President Kennedy's assassination, I wonder whether it was the joke it seemed to be then. As it happened, the threat spurred me into making three hits that day, including a home run with three on after Ewell Blackwell had walked Duke Snider to get to me.

Fear is a two-edged sword that sometimes cuts the wielder. Everyone on Mr. Rickey's staff was quite properly trying to avoid incidents that might call attention to the fact that the Dodger first baseman—I played that position in '47—was a Negro. Harold Parrott, our road secretary, went overboard in his attempts to keep the peace.

Parrott had informed me before our first road trip that I might stay with my teammates in Cincinnati's Netherlands-Plaza Hotel but could not eat in its restaurants. I ordered my meals from room service and ate in my room on an upper floor.

My wife accompanied me on our next western tour. After a game we sat in our room reading the dinner menu. I picked up the phone and asked for room service. "Sorry, Mr. Robinson," said the operator, "there's been a fire in the basement. Room service is shut down today."

The elevators also were out of order, so Rachel and I began the long climb downstairs. Midway we encountered Parrot. "There's a nice hamburger joint down the street, Jack," he said. "You and Mrs. Robinson can eat there." I saw humiliation in Rachel's face. "Come on." I said angrily. "We are going to eat in the grillroom tonight like other guests of this hotel!"

The headwaiter met us at the grillroom door, led us to a table then disappeared. A moment later he returned, a baseball in his hand. "I've been waiting all season for you to come in here, Jackie," he said. He took a pen from his pocket. "I've got every other Dodger's autograph. Will you please sign this ball for me?"

Scouting reports on every Negro with major league potential were in the files at the Dodgers' home office. Mr. Rickey had signed Roy Campanella and Don Newcombe and sent them to Nashua in the New England League. It was obvious that Larry Doby, then with the Newark Eagles of the Negro National League, could easily meet all the requirements of big-league play. But Mr. Rickey was eager to find an ally in his battle for integration and circulated his reports on Larry to other magnates in the hope that someone would sign him.

Says Mr. Rickey:

I was alone in the majors in 1947 as the sponsor of a Negro player until Bill Veeck signed Doby that July. I do not know Veeck's opinion about Negroes at that time, as I never had any conversation with him on the subject. But I can give you my opinion of Veeck's position: he would be the first one in baseball to embrace any innovation, and therefore I would accept him as the one to hire a Negro quicker than anyone I can think of, not because of race, not because he was grappling with a social problem. That would be completely foreign to him. He would not let any tradition interfere with his policy of winning a pennant for his Indians.

After he signed Doby I did advise him to follow the same procedures that I had devised. "Don't allow incidents to happen," I told him. "Control the boy!" Gee, I talked to everyone who did take on a Negro at the start. "Make them agree with you!" I told them. "And convince them that easy-does-it is the right way." I must have said that to Veeck. It wasn't like me not to go to other owners when they hired 'em, and try to tell 'em that my way was best.

Like me, Larry Doby emigrated from the South in his boyhood and won athletic honors above the Mason-Dixon line. Like me, he went to college, spending two years at Long Island University. He was twenty-two, five years younger than me.

Now he was destined to break the color line in the American League.

This is Larry in his own words:

My father worked on a horse-breeding farm at Camden, South Carolina. He died when I was eight and my mother took me to East Orange, New Jersey, to live with her sister. The only work available to her was as a domestic, sleeping in. She enrolled me in a grammar school run by Methodists. The tuition was low and the courses were good. All the money she earned went for my education—many Negro mothers were doing the same thing then.

Truthfully, when I came up North I had no idea that I had been segregated in South Carolina. In the Methodist school in New Jersey the teachers were both white and colored, but all the pupils were Negroes. As far as I was concerned, this was the custom, this was the school, this was it, if you know what I mean.

Later I went to East Side High School in Paterson and became a four-letter man with all-state and all-metropolitan honors in baseball, basketball and football. I was, sort of, the school hero, always one of the crowd, going everywhere with my white schoolmates, parties, dances, shows, what not.

My unconsciousness of discrimination was the same with the Newark Eagles, who signed me in 1943. They paid me about $300 a month—that money looked awful big to me. I was very young and not as conscious of the value of a dollar as I am now. I met with all the discomforts of Negro league life, segregation in hotels and boardinghouses, poor food, and travel on old buses. But we didn't make long jumps. We played in the Philadelphia-Camden area, around New York City or around Virginia, at Norfolk, Newport News and Richmond. Again I thought this was the way things were.

But then I enlisted and wore a U.S. sailor's uniform at Great Lakes Naval Training Station. For the first time I was conscious of discrimination and segregation as never before. It was a shock. If you've never been exposed to it from the outside and it suddenly hits you, you can't take it. I didn't crack up; I just went into my shell. Great Lakes had an all-white ball club with many professional players under Mickey Cochrane's management. I played on an all-Negro team, and lived in segregated quarters. We Negroes included many who were qualified to represent the base. The proof we should at least have had a chance was that we did meet the white team in one game and played them to a standstill, losing, I think, by a 3-2 score. I thought: "This is a crying shame when I'm here to protect my country." But I couldn't do anything about it— I was under Navy rules and regulations and had to abide by them or face the consequences.

After the war Larry returned to the Eagles, where he batted .342 in 1946 and participated in the Negro World Series against the Kansas City Monarchs. He was in a '47 game with the Philadelphia Stars when Lou Jones, publicity director of the Cleveland Indians, told him that Bill Veeck wanted to talk business with him. A few days later Jones met Larry in Chicago's Comiskey Park, where the Indians were about to meet the White Sox. They rode an elevator to an office.

Mr. Veeck greeted me with a big smile and handshake. I said, "I'm glad to meet you, Mr. Veeck." He said, "Call me Bill and I'll call you Larry, Larry." That reassured me, but when he pulled a contract from a drawer and asked me to sign it, I went into a daze.

Then Jones took me down to the clubhouse, where I met Lou Boudreau, the manager. The players were lined up in front of their lockers as if to meet a very important person. Boudreau introduced me to them, one by one. They shook my hand and said a few words, all except Lou Fleming, the first baseman. He turned his back. No one told me what I'd have to face. I was on my own. The Indians treated me like any other rookie. No one made friends with me. I had no roommate on trips. On trains no one invited me to play cards or talk over games. I couldn't stay with the club in the Del Prado Hotel in Chicago. I lived alone in a Negro hotel in St. Louis.

Loneliness made me tense up. Sitting on the bench day after day didn't help. No one seemed to know what I supposed to do on the field. I was used only as a pinch hitter or runner. I struck out a lot because I tried too hard. Fans booed me in St. Louis, Washington and Philadelphia. I worked out at second base and for the first time someone helped me, Joe Gordon, who gave me valuable tips about infield play. My average at the end of the season was 156. I thought I was through, but as I began to pack, Lou Boudreau called me into his office. "Go home and get a good rest, Larry," he said. "When you report at camp next spring we're going to convert you into an outfielder."

I would have been very happy in Tucson the next spring if I'd been able to stay with the rest of the team at the Santa Rita Hotel. The worst thing was not having anyone to communicate with, talk over the game with after it's over and start me thinking about the next game. But I had a wonderful outfield coach, none other than Tris Speaker and by opening day was confident I could play out there. When the opening game began I felt as if everybody was watching just me. I fanned twice. Later that week I made three errors in one game. Then, suddenly, I drove a 450-foot homer over the wall at Griffith Stadium in Washington. They said it was the longest homer ever made there. Newspapermen crowded around me. I began to get over my feeling of depression. The team was clicking. I had a big day in Boston, two singles, a double and a run. But I had days when I kept on striking out. In July I got a big break. Mr. Veeck signed Satchel Paige. I had a roomie at last—and what a roomie! Satch arrived with twenty suits of clothes, a big smile, and no advice except to keep in there playing ball. Satch didn't care what people said or did. All he thought about was baseball.

The Indians headed for a pennant, Larry for a .301 season, capped by six hits in the final series with the Tigers. He led the Indians at bat in the World Series with .318. To all appearances he had eased into white ball with a minimum of difficulty. His tremendous drives—465 feet into the center-field bleachers at Yankee Stadium in May 1949 was the longest—made headlines from coast to coast.

Unpleasant things were happening. I'd gotten accustomed to being jeered at when I failed to come through. Fans are entitled to boo a player when he flops. Like Duke Snider, who was about my age, I still struck out a lot. I had other troubles at the plate. And I was too young to know how to brush off the more serious incidents. A St. Louis fan in a field box yelled names at me from the start of one game. I fanned twice. After I fouled out on my third trip to the plate he leaped from the box and started for me. Satchel picked up a bat to defend me. Hal Peck, a white teammate, grabbed and held the heckler for the cops. That sort of thing would have upset me worse a year earlier, but I was learning how to take hate in stride. Besides, I had friends now.

What hurt more was the way some Cleveland baseball writers turned on me when I committed a boner. We were trailing 7 to 4 in the fifth when we filled the bases with me on third. I watched the pitcher and thought I could get the jump on him as he was winding up for a full delivery. So I lit out for the plate and was called out. The rally was ruined. Stealing home was my own idea. I was overanxious to prove I could do it. But the next day writers I saw every day, guys I kidded with, blasted me as if I'd committed the crime of the century. They as much as said I didn't know the game, didn't know that if I'd scored a run it would have been meaningless, that I couldn't think, couldn't learn, was a moron. The newsmen were entitled to their opinions, I suppose, but not to lie that Lou Boudreau had fined me. Lou did not fine me. He merely said, "Don't do it again, Larry." Muddy Ruel, one of our coaches said, "The best thing to do is to show 'em you can come back after a bad play, Larry." I did. I won the next game with a homer in the ninth.

Muddy talked to me man to man. He said, "If you're on the bench and a fight starts on the field, stay there. Don't put your foot on the grass." He put himself in my shoes. He understood what was happening to me deep inside. And Joe Gordon did everything he could to make me feel comfortable. Looking back I'd say that Joe was a good companion, a pal.

I once checked statistics to find out whether there was any truth in the rumor that Negro players were being thrown at more than whites. The statistics prove it's true, no matter what some of us say. I was knocked down in many games. I was hit more by pitched balls than any player of equal power in the league. Jackie, Campy and Minnie Minoso were also hit repeatedly. We were hit 75 percent more than Joe DiMaggio, Ted Williams or Stan Musial. If a guy wants to brush you back, that's baseball. But head-hunting for Negroes isn't baseball. It's trying to prevent a player from making a living for his family and himself.

My Southern teammates were more reliable than some Northerners. I knew where I stood with them. After they knew me better, they were regular guys on the field. A Northerner might give you the glad hand, but after he discovers that you have as much ability as he, he's a different person altogether.

In 1950 Hank Greenberg became the Indians' general manager and Doby's adviser. Larry had a big year, batting .326 with 102 RBI's and 25 home runs.

That September Cleveland fans gave me a "Night," a Buick and wonderful words. That winter Cleveland baseball writers named me Cleveland's Man of the Hour. In '54, when we again won the pennant, I finished second as the league's Most Valuable Player and led the league in home runs, RBI's and slugging percentage. I was well paid, but didn't get the raise I deserved for that kind of record. I held out for ten days the following spring and was threatened in telegrams with all sorts of things that made me wonder what was going on. Hank hadn't an ounce of prejudice in him. He was trying to keep salaries down, the way all bosses do.

When Bill Veeck became head of the White Sox he got me in a trade. I ended my career with the Indians after another trade in '59.

Most Negroes have just discovered what integration can really mean—I had a touch of it back in '47 and have never stopped learning since. I've learned how to meet and treat with all kinds of people and to respect those who respect me. Economics is at the basis of our problems as Negroes. Education and job opportunities go hand in hand. Anyone who plays big-league ball, Negro or white, has to communicate with all sorts of people in all sorts of circumstances, which is an education in itself. We Negroes try to succeed through necessity; we should try to succeed as our natural right. If we fail, pressure builds up, we become tight, can't relive the pressure and sometimes explode. It's easy for us to talk to other Negroes. What we need is the chance to talk to whites, to explain why we want to get into unions, into motels and hotels and eating places, why we want equality. In baseball we need to explain that we bring dollars into club treasuries while we play, but that when we stop playing our dollars stop. Meanwhile, white players who have been less of a gate attraction get the jobs we deserve.

When I retired in '59 I wanted to stay in the game, to be a coach or in some other capacity, or to manage in the minors until I'd qualify for a big-league job. Baseball owners are missing the boat by not considering Negroes for such jobs. Anyone with wide major league experience knows the fundamentals of the game, the standard of play, and how to get the most out of each man per day. The only way we can make baseball executives understand that we are qualified is to demand that we be given the chance to prove we can lead as well as follow. And there's another field that should be explored: the use of Negroes as sports commentators on radio and TV. Negroes should learn broadcasting techniques in schools. This is a competitive world. The skills and talents of everyone are needed to keep it going. To make baseball stronger, to make the country stronger, the talents and skills of every American, regardless of color, should be used. Baseball was never truly an all-American game until we got into it. This will never be a truly American country until we can compete everywhere on equal terms.

I used to keep my feelings to myself. I wish I'd spoken as I do now. If I had, I'd have been a better ball player.

6

By 1948 Mr. Rickey's plan to put a powerful young Dodger team in the field was progressing smoothly. That June Roy Campanella was brought up from St. Paul, where he had integrated the American Association; Don Newcombe arrived the following May from Montreal. Duke Snider took over the center-field post; Gil Hodges was finally established on first, enabling me to move to my natural position, second base. Pee Wee Reese was a fixture at short, and Billy Cox came from Pittsburgh in the Dixie Walker deal to glove 'em at third. In right was Carl Furillo; left was for grabs. We had half a dozen young strong-armed pitchers plus veteran Preacher Roe.

The little old clubhouse at Ebbets Field rang with our shouts of victory during the years that followed. Captain Pee Wee had two feet more space than anyone around his locker. We often gathered about him in a chorus of Gil's basso, Pee Wee's drawl, Campy's high-pitched laugh, Preach's twang. "Senator" Griffin, our clubhouse attendant, wore a different funny hat for luck as he passed out towels and Cokes each day.

We were all Americans, all teammates, all equal. Leo Durocher briefly occupied the manager's office in '48 after a year in exile, then jumped across the North River to Harlem and the Giants. For a time Burt Shotton sat behind the big desk, then Charlie Dressen, and, finally, Walter Alston. Each treated me and my Negro teammates with absolute fairness. They were not responsible for our lockers being together at Ebbets Field and on the road, a minor form of segregation which escaped the notice of club officials and, for that matter, ours.

There are as many kinds of managers as men. Burt Shotton was the fatherly type. He made everyone feel at ease. But I felt that he was not as good a manager as he might have been because he did not wear a uniform and therefore could not get into the thick of battles for and with his players. Shotton made many fine contributions to baseball. He knew the game, but he was limited in the use of his knowledge by his inability to go on the field. He gave me all the opportunities possible; he treated me exactly the same as everyone else on the ball club, which is as it should be. When I broke in I had a particularly bad streak, but he handled me so wisely that I didn't lose heart.

My experience with Leo Durocher was limited to a few months in 1948 after his suspension was lifted and before he went to the Giants. He impressed me as a man who would use anybody, any tactic, do anything to win. He was a good manager, although without that moral strength which is needed in the handling of young men. His 1963 article in the *Saturday Evening Post* is indicative of what I mean. In it he said much which added up to an interesting story, but the trouble was that many things he reported never happened. I was amazed when I read what he said about incidents in 1947. I first heard of many of these incidents fifteen years after they allegedly happened—and Leo hadn't been with the Dodgers in 1947 after spring training. For example, he mentioned St. Louis as the locale of one incident. In fact he never was in St. Louis that year with the ball club. According to him, he turned on me one day laced me out, using all kinds of racial epithets for the purpose of stirring me up to play better ball. This never happened. He never called me racial names. He may have been thinking such names but he never spoke them. After the publication of his article, he said, "Well, no one has sued me or the *Post*, have they?" I think this is typical of Leo's habit of saying the first thing that comes into his head.

On the other hand, Leo is a great uplifter. He can lift any team out of a losing streak as cleverly as he can pick an unexpected play out of his hat.

I can say nothing but the best of Charlie Dressen. He has been accused of taking all the credit for winning and ducking the responsibility for losing. I disagree. During the years I knew him as my manager we players gave him one hundred percent effort. Charlie would help his worst enemy on the ball club, if the guy could help him win. Charlie's critics have called him "The Great I." I know that Charlie doesn't think of himself personally when it comes to winning ball games. He loves to be responsible for success—but then, who doesn't? He is the ball player's best friend, because he fights for the player's rights.

I didn't blame Charlie for losing the 1951 play-off after we had a 13-game lead. I blame myself and other Dodgers. When our August lead was eleven games I decided that the pennant was in, that we'd break even, pick up a game here and there and finish breezing. So I quit the line-up for a minor operation. In September we had the habit of looking over our shoulders at the scoreboard to see what the Giants were doing, and forgetting to play the team on the diamond. And when the Giants came roaring on, we panicked. This is like America constantly looking over its shoulder to find out what the Soviets are doing when we should concentrate on all the marvelous developments and technical advances in our own country. Charlie Dressen was not responsible for losing that flag. We Dodgers were. As manager Charlie had to take the responsibility and the knocks, whereas we should have spoken up and blamed ourselves.

I used to have managerial ambitions. I don't now. I studied managers' problems while playing. I discovered early that the manager's toughest job is to know how to handle each man as an individual. I couldn't talk to Carl Erskine as I did to Preacher Roe, or Pee Wee Reese. Apart from making decisions on the spot, a manager must know the psychological ups and downs of his players. One of the things Americans must learn is that many Negroes are qualified through experience for managing. Negro players must learn to prepare themselves for managing while still playing. Negroes should accept the idea that this is another color line which must be crossed. George Crowe, Monte Irvin, Ernie Banks and Bill White have earned, by study of the game and its players, the right to consideration as field leaders.

Near our lockers was that of Carl Erskine, one of Mr. Rickey's "fine young men," and a brilliant mound strategist. A writer justly called Carl "the conscience of the Dodgers." He is one of the most fair-minded men I have ever met. He observed our goings-on with the same subtle understanding he applied to the game of baseball. Others might be thinking solely of themselves; he also thought of our problems and tried to put himself in our skins.

Says Carl:

I was born in Anderson, Indiana, were there is no tradition of separation between Negroes and whites. I went to school with Negro boys; one of my closest friends was Johnny Wilson, the Indiana football star who later was a Harlem Globetrotters. As a result, the presence of Negroes on the Dodgers didn't present any problem to me. I didn't appreciate the reasons for the attitude of certain Southern players or of those from other parts of the country who had a different viewpoint from mine.

Jackie Robinson was already established as a big-leaguer in '48, the year I came up. I didn't know a soul on the Dodgers the day I walked into the clubhouse in Pittsburgh. I was uncertain and even scared, for I'd been in baseball only one year. Jackie came over to me right away and welcomed me to the club. He told me he'd seen me in spring training, knew what I could do and that I could help the team. That hit me between the eyes. That got our relationship off the ground on a firm basis and we became friends as time went on.

During those early years I never saw any open resentment toward Jackie, Campy or Don Newcombe. There may have been some by bench warmers, but the Negro Dodgers were all tremendous ball players—when you get a group of guys together in baseball and they're winning, they don't have many gripes, if at all. I think base-ball has handled integration more completely, more lastingly, and with fewer problems than any agency, private or governmental. When you're winning games and shooting for a pennant and you see a guy out there doing what Jackie, Campy and Don did, you want 'em in the line-up.

I remember when Jim Gilliam broke in around '53, some fellows on the club were disgruntled because he wasn't in the line-up every day. When people are pulling together for the same thing, they lose sight of where a man comes from, how he talks or the color of his skin. Gilliam was accepted from the start. Jackie set an example in the earlier years by his self-control. He didn't show outward resent-ment, he didn't retaliate against the vicious baiting from fans and the opposition. He seemed to fight back with more aggressive play at bat and on the bases. There's no question in my mind but that attacks spurred him into playing higher-spirited baseball than he would have played under normal conditions. He had a unifying effect on the team. Pee Wee and Gil playing on either side of Jackie publicly expressed their support of him. In Cincinnati one day someone slid into Jack and shook him up badly. The crowd cheered as he lay on the ground. Gil ran from his position and helped Jack up. Pee Wee, who's extremely well thought of in Cincinnati, walked over to Jack and in a simple gesture, putting his arm about his shoulder, showed those fans that Jack was completely acceptable to him and the other Dodgers, and that that was the way he felt as captain of the team. The cheers stopped. The stands were hushed. It was a great display of comradeship.

I didn't know that Mr. Rickey had given Jackie the go-ahead sign to answer his baiters in '49. I assumed that Jackie had reached a point in his own mind where he had decided to express his opinions openly. We players thought he was justified. He'd kept his feelings pent up too long. We knew he couldn't stay with us in hotels—think of it! . . . the best guy on the ball club! This embarrassed us, for him.

And in the South when Jackie's presence on the team was challenged, when he didn't know whether he would be allowed to play with us, the best player on the team, everyone resented it, too. Whether all of us liked him or not, he was putting money in our pockets and raising our station in life. This is why baseball has successfully integrated: Mr. Rickey picked a qualified player, then gave him the opportunity, and Jack proved he was capable of carrying the load. He helped ease the situation, and helped everyone around him by earning the honors that came his way.

Roy Campanella's outlook was different from Jackie's. Many Negroes have the same ideas Roy had. They experience a measure of success, then say: "Why stir up things? Why get everyone reared up about us?" Roy wanted everyone to be congenial and friendly. He wanted no controversy. When other Negroes on the team complained about their condition, Roy would call 'em into a corner and say, "Look . . . you know where you are, don't you? You're in the big league now. It's nice up here. You're getting an opportunity to show what you can do—don't louse it up for everyone else." Roy had the natural tendency to pour oil on troubled waters. He was critical of Jackie's outspokenness.

I have no doubt that Campy was as sincere in his opinion as Jackie in his. They represented opposite poles of Negro thought about how to effect integration and I respect both, not only as men of high character but as great ball players. Campy caught most of my major league games. We worked together in complete harmony. He was a power, offensively and defensively. I am positive that he has changed with the times, and no longer feels that progress can be made in integration without battling for it.

After '49 when Jackie won the batting championship and Most Valuable Player Award, he was accepted by everyone. There was a lot of kidding, as if the whole idea of segregation had broken down— never anything serious. I don't remember a single open statement against him from the day I reported until the day he quit. As far back as I can remember such guys as Preacher Roe from Arkansas, Billy Cox from Pennsylvania, Billy Loes from New York, and others from other parts of the country, played cards with Jackie, bulled with him. As for social relations off the field, a ball club is composed of twenty-five different individuals. It's very seldom that families get real close or fellows go out together after games.

I don't know the answer to the crisis we're having these days. It's so complex that any solution that seems right has flaws in it from another angle. I'm reaching for words and the word I get is *understanding*. And another, *appreciation* of the other fellow's situation, looking at things from the other side. Jackie is intelligent enough to see the problem from the other side as well as his own. That's what gives him a deeper understanding. As soon as any other Negro came to our ball club, we could understand what it was like for him. We could see it every day. People on the outside couldn't. Some fans said, "There's Negroes on the Dodgers, and I don't root for 'em any more." But when you're on a club with a Negro, you know the guy is flesh and blood, and eats and sleeps, rides a train with you, and sweats with you out there on the field, and he helps your club more than anybody else, and then you walk into a restaurant and they say everybody can eat but him, then you really *understand* what it's like to be a Negro.

Like Campy, Don Newcombe hails from the East Coast. He was born on Staten Island and moved to New Jersey when his father, a chauffer to a real estate dealer, followed his employer to Elizabeth. Mr. Newcombe, Sr. was continuously employed during the Depression at a wage of $45 a week. He worked in a sewing machine factory after the war began.

Don was so big and strong at thirteen that he earned his first dollars as a semipro pitcher who faced batters twice and three times his age. He turned pro at eighteen, joining the fast Newark Eagles:

There was no consciousness of discrimination in my realm of thought when I joined the Eagles. I was a Negro in Negro baseball. Negroes were barred from organized ball and it looked as if the ban would never be lifted. In fact, I was so little interested in white ball that I did not see a big-league game until 1946, when I saw the Yanks and Dodgers play at Yankee Stadium.

The day Mr. Rickey signed Jackie Robinson I was in a movie theater. As I came out I saw big headlines on a newsstand and nearly jumped out of my shoes. I figured I was already good enough to rate a trial with some AAA club. In my early teens, Johnny Grier, my next-door neighbor and a fellow who'd quit Negro ball to become a house painter because the pay was so low, taught me the fundamentals for various pitches and I improved my curve with the Eagles, thanks to Manager Willie Wells, and my catcher Bizz Mackey.

A few months after Jackie's signing, Mr. Rickey bought my contract and I joined Roy Campanella that '46 spring in Nashua in the New England League. That made us the first Negroes in that league. I had little trouble with white players at Nashua because I was so big and they knew I could get back at them with my fast ball. But Campy had to protect himself at all times and was in numerous scrapes. Sal Yvars, who was Manchester's catcher, started a big row by throwing dirty in Campy's face. Pip Kennedy, manager of the Lynn Red Sox, told his players to be rough on Campy, and they got into a fist fight. Buzzy Bavasi, Mr. Rickey's trouble shooter, came up from Brooklyn to prevent the affair from getting out of hand. In that northern part of the country Negroes were more a novelty than bugaboos. Campy won the Most Valuable Player Award and moved up to St. Paul, leaving me as the only Negro on the Nashua team for a while. I had a white roommate, Gus Gallipeau, a French-Canadian semipro hockey player from Pawtucket, Rhode Island. In New England, French-Canadians are looked down on almost as much as Negroes in the rest of the United States. I had two good seasons at Nashua, 14-4 and 19-6, and went to Vero Beach on the Montreal roster in '48. There I encountered

Jackie for the first time. It was only a year since he'd joined the Dodgers, but the effect of his great playing and his restraint could be felt all over the camp. The only trouble I got into in Vero was of my own making. I'd gone to Havana that winter to pick up some extra money pitching. My manager was Mike Guerra, a white Cuban catcher who'd been in organized ball for a long time. Mike wasn't to blame for my wildness; I walked myself out of games and he sent me home. He showed up in Vero on the Athletics, who were playing the Dodgers that day. Being the kind of guy I was then, young and a little hotheaded, I blamed Mike for losing my job in Havana. He was warming up a pitcher in the bull pen when I hollered something to him, forgetting that Mike was considered a white man in Florida and that I was obviously a Negro. We started for each other and were going at it good and hot when a fan yanked loose a picket from the fence and tossed it toward Mike.

"Kill that fresh nigger!" he yelled. Mike walked away and we both shut up.

But the rumor reached the ears of the Mayor and Sheriff of Vero Beach that I'd attacked a white man. They must have been afraid a riot would start the next time I showed up in public. I heard rumors that a plane was waiting to spirit me out of Florida. Well, Mr. Rickey knew me and had confidence in me. In the middle of that night he sent for Jackie, Campy, Sam Jethroe, Buzzy Bavasi and me. We met at his house at 5:30 a.m. We agreed that he should go to the mayor and tell him that I was sorry to have started the row—and I was, for nothing racial was involved. Mr. Rickey said he would confine me to the base to keep me out of trouble with the town people. That ended it except that I got a taste of how Negroes get into nasty scrapes down South that couldn't happen to white men. I admit I'm the kind that strongly resents attacks on my integrity, especially by whites. I'm ready to defend myself against white criticism, whether I'm right or wrong.

No incident involving race prejudice came up during my '48 year in Montreal. The only fight I got into was with a batter I accidentally hit on the hand, putting him out of the game for a few weeks. He was okay by the time we met in Syracuse in the play-offs. I had a 0 and 2 count on him and came in with a fast ball inside. He thought I was trying to hit him deliberately and rushed me, spikes high. I could have swung at him and knocked him cold but didn't. Bobby Morgan and some other Royals pulled him off me. Later, Bill Robinson, the dancer, who was playing a club in Syracuse, called me to his hotel and congratulated me on keeping my head. "You'd have given us a black eye if you'd hit that man," he said. "You must do nothing to give our boys a black eye in baseball." I restrained myself because that's what Jackie was doing. It isn't easy to keep cool when you're being called a "black bastard" or "dirty nigger" and worse. Every time Jackie went to bat against the Phillies, some bench warmer would yell "Knock the black so-and so down!" Jackie acted as if the loud-mouth hadn't been born yet.

I joined the Dodgers on May 5, 1949, about the time that Jackie began to be himself and get into baseball arguments like the rest of the Dodgers. Some thought he was arrogant and went too far. He went no farther than anyone of his temperament would go in the heat of a game. He not only showed Negro players that we could fight for our rights without fear of reprisal; he showed white players he was going to do the same doggone things they did when they thought they were right, even if it meant getting put out of the game. Jackie put umpires, the opposition, and the fans on notice that a Negro was equal in every respect. Liberal-minded fans understood this. The others were learning. I had to take abuse, too, although not one-millionth of what Jackie took. The Phillies' trained parrot got after me every time I faced that team. After I was traded to Cincinnati in '58 I was a teammate of Del Ennis, who'd been a Philly in my early days in the league. He told me that one day he went over to the hired baiter and said, "You'd better leave that son of a bitch Newcombe alone. I've got to bat against him! Let me get out of the game with my bat before that tongue of yours gets him mad!" I got threatening crank letters every once in a while, like Jackie got a letter warning him he'd be shot in a Cincinnati double-header. How could anyone get so crazy as to think a nutty letter could scare us out of baseball?

By '49 the air was already clearing. After '50 a new kind of player came up to the Dodgers. Young fellows with a different outlook. We still stayed by ourselves, didn't want to socialize with them. We ate in our rooms in St. Louis and Cincinnati. We'd sit together in dining rooms in other cities, go to the movies together or to the homes of people we knew. Later on, we went with white players whenever we and the whites wanted to do the same things. We were actually segregated only in clubhouses, where our three lockers were always side by side. We three alternated in sharing hotel rooms. Sometimes Campy would bunk with Jackie, sometimes I would, the odd man having a room to himself.

Our only real kick was during training in the South and in border cities where we would have to separate from the rest of the club on road trips. In St. Louis we lived in a Negro hotel that was all right for its time. But there was no air conditioning and we'd lie awake suffocating all night. I often wonder how we played as well as we did on little if any sleep. Many a time we soaked our sheets in cold water or hung our heads out of windows for a breath of fresh air. Jackie ended all of that. He was man enough to go to the Chase Hotel and beef to the manager. The manager told him it was all right to sleep in the Chase, but we couldn't use the hotel's swimming pool. Jackie said, "We don't want to use your swimming pool—none of us knows how to swim." That's how segregation ended at the Chase. I don't think many of these young kids now in the big leagues know how this was done.

As time went by we Negroes were making our mark in baseball, winning Rookie and Most Valuable Player Awards, batting championships and other honors. White players realized we were doing a hell of a job for baseball. By 1958, big-league ball players knew in their hearts that complete integration was inevitable. In his later Dodger years Jackie was a regular in mixed card games; Campy went fishing with white Dodgers in Florida each spring. Carl Furillo, who'd signed the petition against Jackie in Panama, came to me and said, "Don, I was forced to sign that thing by the others. I never read it— I'm sorry I did it." Pee Wee Reese is one of the finest gentlemen I've ever met in baseball. Whatever feelings he might have had against Negroes before Jackie's time, and I don't know whether he had any, certainly were never evident to me. Preacher Roe never said or did anything detrimental to the advancement of Negroes in baseball. Billy Cox was more outspoken than Preach, but only about baseball as it's played; he was one of the card-playing crowd that Jackie belonged to. Duke Snider was all baseball, too. When he was hitting he was everybody's pal; when he slumped he was hard to approach, nasty to everyone. I never knew how to figure Duke out—he was from California and we never knew how to figure Californians—some hated Negroes, others were the fairest-minded people in the country. Gil Hodges is from Indiana, like Carl Erskine. He's as much of a gentleman as Reese, which means he was always our friend.

As for my managers—Shotton, Dressen, Alston—none had any animosity in their hearts toward Negroes. Each played his own kind of ball. Shotton was an old man and not well. I shall always remember Shotton as the one who helped me most as I broke into the big leagues. He pitched me in St. Louis a few days after I was called up from Montreal—and I got bombed. As I came back to the dugout I expected him to hand me a train ticket back to Montreal. Instead, he came running to me, shook my hand and said, "Big fellow, don't you worry. I'm starting you in Cincinnati on Sunday." He did, and I threw a shutout. I was twenty-one, a Negro and worried sick about making good. His words made the big difference between losing my confidence and becoming a winner. In my wildest dreams I'd never believed I'd be out there on the mound, pitching against the Musials and the Slaughters, playing beside Reese and Hodges. Burt Shotton made me a member of the team. Charlie Dressen won our respect because he knows what he's talking about when it comes to baseball. Ball players are prone to second-guess their managers. Not Charlie Dressen. We had confidence in him and he had confidence in us. We didn't blame him for losing the '51 play-off. We blamed ourselves. When I tired in the ninth inning of the last game with Bobby Thomson coming up, I remembered Charlie coming to the mound and asking me how I felt. "Talk to Pee Wee and Jackie," I said. "They've been watching my stuff. They know how much I've pitched in the last week. Call Campy, too." They all met at the mound. Jackie said, "Big fellow, how do you feel?" "I'm tired," I said, "but I'll give it all I can." Dressen said Clyde Sukeforth had phoned him from the bull pen that between Branca and Labine, Ralph was throwing the hardest. That's how it happened. Then Branca replaced me and Thomson hit that homer.

Nothing changed after Mr. Rickey resigned in 1950 and went to Pittsburgh. His organization remained intact under Mr. O'Malley. Buzzy Bavasi was directly in charge of the club. He was supposedly in our corner. I was the top pitcher. Changes in ownership or management made no difference to me. I was satisfied with the money I was getting. I didn't get a promised raise for winning twenty games in '51, because I was going in the Army. But the same might have happened to a white 20-game winner. The Dodgers were tops to us.

In 1955 Don put all his savings into a package liquor store and cocktail lounge in Newark. "Any business that lasts as long as mine must be a success," he says. After a winning season with the Reds in 1959 his fast ball lost its zip, and when his back bothered him the following year he retired from active play.

Carl Erskine
Photo courtesy of National Baseball Hall of Fame Library, Cooperstown, NY.

7

"I knew what I was the first time I looked down at my arm and saw my skin," says Roy Campanella. "I knew what my father was, white—and a wonderful man—and what my mother was, black and a wonderful woman. Thank God, both of 'em are still living."

Campy was a Negro National League veteran at twenty-five when Mr. Rickey signed him in 1946. In his boyhood he had ridden the streets of Philadelphia on his Italian father's vegetable cart, a gregarious boy with a sunny, outgoing disposition. He had been earning $3,000 a year with the Baltimore Elite Giants ("as good a team as many in the majors") when Mr. Rickey sent him to Nashua at half that salary. "Some people—I don't know who they are—may think that I didn't fight for my rights hard enough in those days," he says. "Well, it was hard for me to know how because I was in a position no one had been before." Then, defiantly: "I never was a clown!"

Today's Roy Campanella, victim of a tragic motor accident, sits in an office in his busy Harlem liquor store and reminisces:

It's a horrible thing to sit here and realize what a situation like this means to an individual—to be born an American and have to go to court to find out how much of an American he is. It's a horrible thing to be born in this country and go along with all the rules, laws and regulations and have to battle in court for the right to go to the movies—to wonder which store my children can go in in the South to try on a pair of shoes or where to sleep in a hotel. I am a Negro and I am part of this. I don't care what anyone says about me . . . I feel it as deep as anyone, and so do my children.

I thought as major league ball players we who first integrated baseball had done a lot for Negroes. Well, we didn't even scratch the top of the cake. If life in general was a baseball game in the National or American League, this country wouldn't have these problems today. If every Negro in the United States could live as we did in the National League, what a country this would be! Yes, we had our problems, but nothing compared to what's outside this building today. If whites and Negroes could live together and get along together as we did on our ball club, play together, want to win together, lose together, and, after the ball game, you go your way, I go my way, there'd be no dead little girls in Birmingham or thousands in jail today. If my teammates didn't want to go with me socially, that was okay; we still had things in common. The next day, when we got on the field, we had only one objective—to win. We treated each other accordingly.

How was this done? Well, there was one man, Mr. Rickey, that had this idea of integration, and had faith in it—and stuck his neck out. A lot of others went along with him later, but it was his idea; he stayed with it until it was more than an idea. Thank God he did! He showed the world that Negroes had ability plus—and could be gentlemen, too.

I broke into organized ball in New England, which was a part of the country where integration wasn't necessary—there weren't any Negroes in Nashua when Don Newcombe and I played there. We ran into difficulties in Lynn, Massachusetts. They had a manager down there who didn't particularly care to see Negroes in the league. He did his utmost to try to dishearten us. But when someone tries to dishearten you—I know I was like this and so was Newcombe—you'd try just that much harder. And you when you try harder it improves your ability. It was the same with Jackie—the more they criticized Jackie or tried to hurt him, the better his performance was. That's the key to all of these Negro athletes' performances. Baiting may hurt some, but their opponents soon find out that by riding 'em they make 'em perform better. So they decide, "We better leave these fellows alone."

Mr. Rickey sent me to St. Paul to open up the American Association. I had some incidents there. I'd never played in Louisville before, and had some catcalls and that sort of thing—it wasn't too bad. My first series there I did some good hitting, and that stopped the riders. When you stick a thorn in the other side's side it puts a stop to this racial hatred stuff. It makes some people take notice that you're not running to the hills because they say "Boo!" A display of ability overshadows those hoots from people in the stands. They even start admiring you.

I was prepared when I went to the Dodgers in '48. I'd been lectured by Mr. Rickey. He told me to just about expect anything, and I did. He lectured me on putting on my best performance in the field at all times. He told me to always be a gentleman off the field. These were the main things, he said.

Now, when it comes to the way I acted as a Dodger, it wasn't that I was different from Jackie or that I had a different personality or philosophy. It was my position, catching. A catcher has to make people like him, no matter what. My God, if a catcher didn't go to an infielder or outfielder and say, "Look, you're playing a little out of position," what kind of catcher would he be? A catcher has to take charge. He has to say, "We're pitching this man different," or say, "You're not pitching this man right." I had to go to everyone on the team. An outfielder can't go to a pitcher and say he's pitching a man wrong. The pitcher'll say, "Who the heck does this outfielder think he is?" But from a catcher he would accept that criticism. I thought of myself as a catcher first, not as a Negro. I don't think I acted that way because my father was white or that I came from Philadelphia in the North or because I had a cheerful disposition. I based my attitude purely on that I was a catcher. If I wasn't a catcher I don't think I'd have gone to players on the club and told them what I did. I was like a quarterback in football who's running the ball club. In professional ball they let you know this early. I'd played a lot of years in professional ball. They may not have considered the Negro leagues were as good as the big leagues but in my opinion our colored league was a real top league. I had played in that league nine years. I knew something about catching. I'd handled some fine pitchers. I knew I had to take charge when I was there on that field. I don't care what kind of league I'd play in, I had to be a take-charge catcher. I knew everything about my pitchers and about my infielders. I controlled my pick-off plays. I placed my outfielders where I thought the hitters would be hitting in the wind. And I directed the pitchers to pitch to them so they would be hitting that way. So being that kind of catcher, I had to make everyone on the team work with me. I had to have a sunny disposition, I had to keep the tempo up. You can't be demanding. You got to have a piece of sugar in your hand. I thank the good Lord that I was made the way I am, and that I've never had a harsh remark back from anyone who said, "Well, who the hell are you, telling me off!" Any pitcher I've caught, white or colored, knew what I meant, and that was my job, to be the best catcher in baseball, and a Negro. And a jolly fellow, that's all.

Jackie and I were different kinds of people. So was Pee Wee Reese; his personality was different from Jack's and Duke Snider's. These are all different people. They think different. They act different. But all of us had one objective—to win. And that brought us together, no matter what color.

It's not the Supreme Court decision about schools that made me realize about the other things in Negro life. It's what happened since then that's made a lot of individuals realize, who didn't think like that before. My God, a lot of people who've never been in the South and don't know these things exist, to hear the governors of these different states and senators from these different states publicly say the things they do on television or on radio across the world. . . . This has never been brought out before. Every Negro in the South knew how they'd acted, and went along because they had to—these modern-day cave men who run the South to come out openly and say the slanders they say on television and radio—I think it's ridiculous, shameful! The whole world knows it now and it's a big pill for the United States to swallow. To say that the American Negro has been free for one hundred years and, my God, he can hardly vote in the South, is that being free? He's born in America and not a real American. . . . I sit here and listen and see these governors, and hear the statements they make—educated men, leaders . . . leaders of people . . . to come out openly and say the harsh things they say against us Negroes—what do these leaders want? My God, when a Negro's born into this world . . . and a little white boy today, he's born into this world . . . the little white boy will never have to worry about going to court to prove how much of an American he is! He's born an American, but a little Negro boy, he has to fight his battle to find out how much of an American he is. And that's exactly what this is all about.

I'm in business here in New York. I have to abide by the white man's law. I pay all the taxes, I withhold Social Security from my employees. I take my receipts to the bank to deposit, the same as any white businessman would do. But if I go to certain places, if I go South I can't go to a public park. I'm paying the same taxes as a white man but if my children go down South—and they've been with me down South in spring training—they can't eat wherever they want, or go to a public park in many places, or swim in a swimming pool. This is not what you call justice. And without justice what kind of country is this?

I'm not a politician. I'm not a leader. I was a baseball player. I've tried to do everything I can for my people. We've got the integration ball rolling now. As I say, it's a big pill and it's a tough one for them to swallow. The leaders of this country have to do something or they'll choke on it. They just have to . . . you can't have this many people and tell them that they're not Americans. That's what they're telling us. We thought we were accomplishing a lot when we integrated baseball. We never thought it would be like this. I didn't think this would go for years and years and years. I thought this would gradually change. It did gradually change in baseball. We fellows thought we were accomplishing something. We didn't think it would be like it is today. Mr. Rickey said there'd be no segregation at Vero Beach. But if you leave out Dodgertown, we were segregated everywhere. I thought conditions would gradually change, and they did. At first we were not allowed in the Chase Hotel in St. Louis, then we were. In Philadelphia, that's my home town, I never stayed at the hotel—it was segregated, too—but that changed.

I spoke up the first time I rode in a Dodger bus and couldn't go in a restaurant in West Palm Beach. I told 'em I'd be damned if I wanted to ride with 'em again. That was the first year I was with the Dodgers. Jackie wasn't with us; he had a car and left early. Branca came out and asked me if I wanted a sandwich. I said, "No, I don't want a sandwich. I'll wait until I get to Vero Beach, but I'll be damned if I get in another bus and ride any place." I told that to the road secretary, Harold Parrott. "From now on," I said, "make arrangements so I can get a car so I won't be embarrassed sitting in a bus while the others eat. I'm not sitting in any kitchen to eat, either!" And they got me a car.

Negro players in the game today have a different philosophy from what we fellows did. When we started, when anyone starts something, they're uneasy. You don't know how things will turn out. You're expecting something you may not get. Nowadays the Negro that has the opportunity to play major league baseball, he knows all he has to do is act like a gentleman and to have the ability. If there's something wrong he can speak up whenever he sees something's wrong and not get crucified for it.

Every Negro in the country is affected by what's going on. The black man all over the world is affected, too. Everyone has his eye on these civil rights bills and laws and demonstrations. Things are at a higher point than ever before. Things have been brought into the open that a lot of people never knew about before. This struggle has mushroomed into something more powerful than the hydrogen bomb. This is the biggest explosive the United Sates has. They can't put it in a blanket and tie a knot around the head of it. It's in the open and it'll never be closed up again. That's exactly the way I feel about it. I have two young sons in school that this struggle will affect later on. I'm giving them the best education I can. I think that education to the colored man is the greatest asset in the world. We're coming. Don't forget this—the colored man is much better qualified than he was ten years ago.

Sitting here I have a lot of time to read and watch different programs and to be much more aware of things than when I was playing. I thank God that we Negroes are moving forward instead of backwards.

✳

$\mathcal{T}$he future of integrated baseball was still uncertain in 1948. Conservative club owners regarded Branch Rickey as "that man on Montague Street" who was always trying to upend the status quo, while Bill Veeck was a maverick they wanted to get out of their sight. The next breach in the wall of segregation came when Horace Stoneham signed Monte Irvin and Hank Thompson, veterans of the Negro National League.

The Giants had been in financial difficulties during the war. Outsiders suggested that Stoneham was signing Negroes in order to attract fans to the Polo Grounds from nearby Harlem. As time proved, Stoneham has been a powerful agent in advancing the cause of integration, not that such was his original purpose. "We were merely looking for the best possible talent," says Charles S. Feeney, Stoneham's nephew and currently the Giants vice president.

Stoneham's big prize was Irvin, a star of high character and intelligence. Monte was a thunderous hitter whose drives had landed in the stands near the clubhouse office during Negro National League games. The Giants sent him to Jersey City, their AAA farm club, in the spring of '49. There he hit an extraordinary .510 in 18 games with 10 home runs and 24 RBI's. Overnight he became a Giant:

Monte Irvin, the man, speaks here:

I was born in Alabama but my family moved to New Jersey when I was six. We lived in an integrated neighborhood in Orange. The boys I knew were rough and tough, the kind that become juvenile delinquents in their teens. I turned to sports to work off my excess energy rather than hang around street corners. I played soccer in grade school, then went into baseball, football, basketball and track, developing my body and mind.

My father is a heroic figure to me. He worked long hours in a dairy to support my mother and us kids on Depression pay of $18 to $20 a week. It takes patience, energy and love to bend your back to that kind of effort.

There was good feeling between white and Negro boys in Orange. We played together, fought together and had good times together. In 1932 I joined the Orange Triangles, a mixed team in a mixed league. I was an oversized kid with plenty of baseball talent. The Triangles played twilight games beginning at five o'clock, for we sold papers and ran errands to earn pennies during the day. We drew big crowds that paid 25 cents each—that's how we got the money to pay for our equipment and uniforms. It was good fun, no unpleasantness, boys of all nationalities in a fine relationship, thanks to baseball.

My parents often spoke about conditions in the South. It was disheartening to hear how poorly they'd lived. They thought that ball-playing against white teams was great progress. It was a sort of progress, but in Orange certain restaurants, stores, and places of entertainment did not welcome Negroes. Since then Orange has undergone a metamorphosis in this respect, but much more improvement is necessary before complete tolerance can be enjoyed.

I was eighteen when I joined the Newark Eagles. Players of tremendous talent were in the Negro leagues. We lived in a little world within a big one, citizens of an underprivileged nation of Negroes. I was paid $125 a month at the start. Each team owned a bus. We Eagles might play in Newark one day, in Kansas City two days later, in Birmingham the next day, sleeping on the bus as it jogged over bad roads, a dollar a day for meal money. It was late in the Depression when I started, and a dollar paid for one real good meal a day. We'd dig into our pockets when we were really hungry.

In big cities we'd stay in Negro hotels or in furnished rooms elsewhere, rent paid by the club.

We envied white players who could rise as their ability permitted, but we didn't talk much about such things, not even about not making a decent living. The hard blow was to our pride, not being able to prove that we were just as good as the whites, that many us of could have added lines to the records books if we'd had the chance. I spent five years with the Eagles, then went overseas to England, France and Germany as a private in a Negro engineering outfit. I returned after the war a buck sergeant and went back to the Eagles. I was playing winter ball in Cuba to make enough to live on when a Giants scout saw me.

That first spring training with the Giants organization I'd climb into the club bus with my teammates for a trip, say, from our Sanford base to Daytona Beach. Midway the bus would stop before a restaurant. White players would go in, buy me sandwiches and bring them out to me. My teammates stayed overnight in a hotel; I slept in a Negro rooming house, even in Sanford. Joe Becker, our Jersey City manager, would say, "Fortunately, you'll be out of this part of the country soon." This didn't salve my feelings. I was contributing my share to the club, and had no doubt that I would make good. Most of my teammates sympathized with me, for segregation made no sense to them either. Frankly, I hated my situation.

In Southern ball parks I was subjected to the same kind of name-calling that greeted high-school students in Little Rock and college students in Mississippi and Alabama in recent years—and not only in the South, as I learned when I became a Giant. I retaliated by playing harder, taking out my anger in base hits. When I arrived in the Polo Grounds for the first time, Leo Durocher was the manager. He called me into his office. "You're on the Giants now," he said. "I want you to feel at home. You'll get no special favors and so will nobody else. Try to relax and make the team." The Giants, among them some Southerners, were nice to me. Leo and other members of the Giants organization wouldn't stand for discrimination if they could prevent it. This made for good team spirit. Besides, Jackie Robinson had paved the way for us. By '49 the pitfalls were pretty well known.

Often I'm asked, "What about after games? Did you socialize with white players?" Well, there's small chance of social life for any kind of ball players. Big-leaguers are family men. They want to drive home as quickly as possible after games and socialize with their wives and kids. On the road it was the individual's choice whether he wanted to join his teammates at restaurants or the movies.

We were housed with the team in the two border cities of St. Louis and Cincinnati. We had been segregated at the Chase Hotel in St. Louis at first but Jackie broke down the ban. Baseball was the first to desegregate many hotels—it's been involved in many firsts long before the present civil rights campaign. We Negro Giants desegregated the Adams Hotel at our Arizona training base in Phoenix. At first the dining room and swimming pool was closed to us. Phoenix was then an almost completely segregated city. One night Kenny Washington and I went to a movie theater. Kenny had been All-American in football with Jackie at UCLA. He and Bob Waterfield, the most popular football player in South California, were intimate friends. Kenny had also played small parts in pictures. He took for granted that he was a full American citizen. But that movie theater wouldn't sell us tickets. It was a disillusioning experience for him. He never quite got over it.

The same thing happened to Willie Mays in Phoenix. I can't for the life of me understand why I and the others, including Willie, didn't protest more than we did. If we had, the situation might have been remedied much sooner.

In '54 the Giants and Indians barnstormed through the South on an exhibition tour. There were five Negroes on the Indians and four on the Giants. The two teams ate together, slept in the same hotels on the first leg of the trip and had a hell of a good time. Then we reached cities in the Deep South. When we arrived at a railroad station there'd be a bus for the white players, while we had to wait around with our bags until a Negro cabdriver came along, which might be half an hour or more. We were tired, then disgusted, then bitter, knowing how much we were contributing to our teams and baseball. "We ought to quit this team until it hits New York," we'd tell each other. But we never did. We weren't concerned with our civil rights; we were concerned with our comfort. We should have tried to correct injustices as they arose. If you sit around waiting for something to fall into your lap, you're likely to get hit in the head.

We complained about discrimination in St. Petersburg the year we trained there. We had to stay at a boardinghouse with one toilet. White players had individual hotel rooms, individual toilets; they ordered dinner from a full menu card. We ate whatever was shoved before us. They had but one idea—to make the team. We had to worry about our rest, our diet, how to get to the ball park, where to relax after games, which store door to open as we walked down the main street. We complained to Eddie Brannick, who is still the Giants' road secretary. "Well, boys," he said, "it's just too bad, but there's nothing I can do about it—it's the local law." I believe that Ford Frick, the league presidents and club owners should have acted then. They should have told Southern segregationists that Negroes were contributing hell of a lot to baseball and to business places in Southern towns. They should have told them that high-salaried Negro stars were suffering indignities that no white man would tolerate.

Even today when ball clubs are buying hotels and motels to avoid segregation during spring training, most Negroes dread going South to see those WHITE ONLY signs. Baseball is in a position to bring economic pressure on Southern towns which enforce segregation. Club owners should threaten to abandon spring training sites where Negroes lose their status as human beings the moment they put a foot on a sidewalk.

*

In common with every player who participated in Negro ball before the war Monte is insistent that recognition be given the great stars of those days. He chased Josh Gibson's mammoth drives; he faced Satchel Paige's fireballs:

How many know that Josh hit seventy home runs in 1940? Or that Satch sometimes pitched seven times a week? Who knows that Buck Leonard could hit as hard and often as Lou Gehrig? Or about Hilton Smith, Terris McDuffie, Billy Byrd, Jonas Gaines? All might have been 20-game winners in the majors. Ray Dandridge was forty when he played in Minneapolis with me, and a better third baseman you never saw. In the course of a season Dandridge seldom made more than one or two errors; he came in on swinging bunts, grabbed the ball barehanded, threw to first without looking, and got his man! Willie Wells, who played shortshop with me on the Eagles, worked a play never seen today—the second baseman crossed the bag to his right, grabbed a ground ball while Willie crossed to his left, took the ball on a short toss and fired to first for a 4-6-3 putout! And Cool Papa Bell who'd bunt his way on, light out for second on a sacrifice along the third-base line and fly around second to third without stopping. Of course it's been done in the majors, by Ty Cobb and Jackie, but when was the last time you saw it? Bell took the extra base on a sacrifice, consistently upsetting the infield with his speed. He was faster than Maury Wills or Sam Jethroe—and as clever with the bat as Richie Ashburn.

I could go and on . . . it's a crime no one important on the white side saw them in action or recorded their feats. I remember the year Satchel Paige's All-Stars met Joe DiMaggio's white major-leaguers in the California winter league. Joe's boys would come over and say, "It's a shame you fellows can't play with us—you'd make it easily." Joe himself said Satchel was the greatest pitcher he'd ever faced. The Homestead Grays used to outdraw the Senators at Griffith Stadium in Washington. The Grays had Josh Gibson, Buck Leonard, Roy

Partlow and Raymond Brown—any one of whom could have helped the Senators get out of the cellar. Roy Campanella asked for a tryout with the Phillies in the early '40s and was turned down. This shows how self-defeating segregation is!

Monte reached the peak of his career in the 1951 World Series with the Yankees. His four hits in the first game, his eleven hits in a six-game Series, his ten singles, and his theft of home in the first game were brief flashes of baseball genius.

That fall the Essex County Democratic organization nominated him for the New Jersey Assembly.

It was an unexpected honor, but I was unable to campaign, for I'd already contracted for a barnstorming tour. I'd made little money until then and couldn't afford to stump. But I did circulate my platform. I believe in tolerance not only for Negroes but for anyone, and by that I mean equality in all things. I wanted to see more housing projects for low-income families, and slum clearance. I was for more playgrounds in slums, so that there'd be fewer juvenile delinquents. And I wanted the narcotics laws to be enforced. Unfortunately Essex was a Republican county, so I wasn't elected.

From long experience Monte offers advice to Negro big-leaguers:

They should save as much money as they can while still in the game. I advise active players to obtain expert advice from honest businessmen before they invest their money. Many a player has lost his savings by plunging into businesses with unstable futures.

I am confident that jobs will open one day for Negro umpires, coaches and managers, but only after the entire country is reconciled to granting equal rights to all. Right now among retired and active players are Negroes with backgrounds suited to these jobs. Owning a package liquor store, bowling alley or selling insurance is hardly the vocation for an athlete who has accumulated a lifetime knowledge of the game. Every Negro player—and, for that matter, every Negro—should keep up with the civil rights struggle and help wherever he can. Negro players should speak up privately and publicly. Wrongs they may be suffering should be brought into the open. America is a wonderful country because Americans may legally petition for the redress of wrongs.

I've traveled in many other countries; I know we have more of everything here, including the right to speak freely. There's still a lot of wrong in the United States. The only way to guarantee the righting of these wrongs is education, the ability to understand and to say what you know to be right. This country is big enough, there's enough wealth and opportunity here for everyone, including 20,000,000 Negroes. Until we are integrated into the whole structure of American society, America can never be wholly free. The test of a man's merit should be his ability—if a Negro has the ability to be President of the United States he should be considered for the post. If a Negro has the ability to be manager of the Giants he should be considered for that post.

America will be a healthier country in the future because of the civil rights struggle now going on. We Negroes have already lifted America from the pessimism and defeatism of postwar years. We have made other Americans recall the ideals this nation was founded on, the Constitution as it was written, not as it is misinterpreted by some. We've made other Americans think.

Ball players used to be concerned only with hits or pitching a winning game. Now that Negroes are hitting and pitching on the same fields as whites the whites are learning from them that every man should be treated equally. Sports has done more to prove that democracy works than all the angry blast-offs and speeches in Congress about states' rights, property rights, and the rights of everyone and everything but Negro rights. Negro athletes—Jackie in baseball, Joe Louis in boxing, Wilt Chamberlain in basketball, Jim Brown in football, and all those record holders in track—they've brought honor to America, the same America that the segregationists downgrade.

I've got a dream about solving this problem of integrating the Deep South. I'd like to see a star quarterback, one of those passing, running, kicking kids, become the University of Alabama's all-American—and he's a Negro! I can see the student body rising up en masse if anybody tries to railroad him out because he's a Negro!

Then, on a personal note, Monte says:

Take this kid Ed Kranepool, now with the New York Mets. He's eighteen and, in my opinion, has the makings of a star. I was eighteen once, a big, strapping fellow with tremendous athletic potentialities. Think what I might have been if I'd had Kranepool's opportunity at eighteen. I don't mean the bonus money I didn't make. I mean the satisfaction of fulfilling my ambitions, of being a complete man.

When I was in the Army I took basic training in the South. I'd been asked to give up everything, including my life, to defend democracy. Yet when I went to town I had to ride in the back of a bus, or not at all on some buses. It doesn't make sense to waste the energy and brains of millions of Negroes because a minority doesn't like people with darker skins than theirs. It doesn't make sense that these bigots cheer a Negro athlete and accept him as an equal as long as he wears the home-town uniform. The obstructionists need a strong dose of commoner sense.

Baseball has done more to move America in the right direction than all the professional patriots with their billions of cheap words. Baseball has proved that it can be done.

In my opinion, it surely will be done!

PART II

The Present

Nature, with equal mind,
Sees all her sons at play. . . .
—Matthew Arnold

9

By 1951 integration was accepted as a way of life in baseball except in a few backward quarters. Colored Latin Americans joined their white compatriots. By 1959 colored players were on every big-league team.

In 1963 51 Negroes and 24 colored Latins were in the majors, or 15 percent of the total. Among them were five former batting champions, six Rookies of the Year, and six MVP's. Ten of eleven leading National League batters were nonwhites; as were three of the first ten American League batters. Tommy Davis won the older circuit's batting crown for the second consecutive year; Maury Wills was again the majors' top base stealer.

Not one incident of a racial nature marred play. All clubs had desegregated training facilities, with the exception of the Minnesota Twins, who yielded to pressure from local fans and were preparing to unite their entire squad under the same roof in 1964.

Organized baseball's policy toward integration and related problems is discussed by Commissioner Ford C. Frick in this taped interview:

Baseball's function is not to lead crusades, not to settle sociological problems, not to become involved in any sort of controversial racial or religious question. The function of baseball is to produce the best games possible and to pick its players solely on their ability to run, hit, throw, to play the game. And that is the way this integration situation was really approached.

We must remember that we are talking about a sport of which organized baseball is but a single facet. By its very nature baseball lends itself to interest on the part of all sorts of people. Nothing about the game requires the use of players of a certain race or creed or color, size, stature, or degree of education. Some sports, by their very nature, are limited. Golf, for instance, is an expensive game. The average youngster of Little League age cannot afford to play golf. Certain other games require much equipment or certain physical types. Baseball is a most democratic game because it does not distinguish between individuals. The only thing baseball is interested in is performance.

Baseball evolved in slavery days. Colored people did not have a chance to play it then, and so were late in developing proficiency. It was more than fifty years after the introduction of baseball before colored people in the United States had a chance to play it. Consequently, it was another fifty years before they, by natural process, arrived at the state where they were important in the organized baseball picture. And as quickly as they attained that importance organized baseball began to show an interest in them, not as crusaders or because we were trying to solve the racial problem but simply because a new field was opening up where great talent existed.

A lot of people want to know how our interest in colored players come about. It was not sudden. You must remember that from 1918 to the end of the Second World War we had gone through serious economic and military situations. Many of our players went to war. Many were injured and couldn't come back; others were forced out of baseball by economic necessity. We became more and more interested in finding talent elsewhere. At that time baseball was developing in Cuba and other Latin-American countries, where there was no color distinction, where colored ball players had a great opportunity to develop. Consequently, they offered us a great deal of playing strength. Baseball saw the opportunity and took it.

Now, baseball is a typically American game, a combination of team effort and individual play. The American way of life is equally a combination of team effort and individual choice. Because baseball was established during slavery days it lagged behind in using colored players. Baseball's breaking of the color line reflected changes taking place in the country at large. In other words, baseball was not a front-runner in breaking the color line. Its tardiness in this respect was inherent in the attitude of American society, while the strength of America was equally the strength of baseball. Baseball has been an integral part of the evolution of American society. We are an institution as well as a game; we have had all the difficulties in finding solutions that any institution of our scope must have.

Baseball has done a wonderful job of integration not because we had an axe to grind but because the path was indicated to us. Negroes wanted something. Baseball had that something to give them. To accept it they had to meet the requirements set up by us not in a campaign for integration but because, to present our product properly to the public, we had to formulate certain rules. Baseball has had to make sacrifices to meet this demand. For years one of our strongest leagues was the Southern Association. It embraced the great cities of Birmingham, New Orleans, Atlanta, Memphis, Mobile, Shreveport, Nashville and Little Rock. We suddenly arrived at the point where the colored player was important to baseball. He was doing a tremendous job and we needed him. The Southern Association was in territory where state laws forbade integration. Something had to give.

Baseball could not afford to change its policy for a few Southern cities. We had to say to the Southern Association, "We're sorry—we can't put teams with colored players in some of your towns. We cannot change our policies to meet the standards of local laws." We never held joint major league meetings where sixteen club owners or their representatives sat down and voted Yes or No on this subject. It was handled much more simply; it was handled individually. Where we couldn't use colored players, we didn't go into those towns. Major league teams canceled games in spring training because they were not permitted to use their colored players.

In a Dixie play-off for the Little World Series some years ago a Texas team was scheduled to play in a town where colored players could not be used. After a conference between the Commissioner and representatives of the American Association we decided to ask the teams not to play the games. They asked us if they could substitute white players for colored. We said, "You play your players as they are or you don't play at all." Fortunately the club in the Southern Association that was giving us the trouble got licked and failed to qualify for the Little World Series. The following year play-off games in segregated towns were called off.

Georgia once had such a law, but it no longer exists. Alabama still has segregation laws in ball parks, and therefore no organized baseball today. Little Rock was without baseball after the Southern Association disbanded. Who started the drive for a team there in 1963 I don't know. Suddenly there was a surge of interest in restoring the game. Little Rock's businessmen wanted to get a team in the American Association, but the American Association was about to break up. Under the leadership of Ray Winder a committee was formed with the idea of getting Little Rock into the International League. We told him that we would try to give him a franchise provided Negroes were accepted in Little Rock. Well, you know how Little Rock was about integrating the schools. Now its businessmen agreed that Negroes on other International League teams could play in Little Rock, and the city returned to baseball. And on the new Little Rock team was Richie Allen, a fine young Negro player.

The local folks expected trouble. On opening day the park was picketed—by just one man. Governor Faubus himself threw out the first ball. The next day the one-man picket line failed to show up, and has never been seen since. And colored players now play there in every game without any problems whatsoever.

About segregation in Southern towns during spring training, it's been handled individually by major league clubs. John Quinn told me that the hotel in Clearwater, Florida, where the Phillies train, drew the color line. The Phillies solved the problem very simply—they moved out of the hotel. There was no bitterness, just the Phillies saying, "You don't want colored players, do you? Well, we'll go where they do." The team moved to a motel on the causeway between Clearwater and Tampa. Fifteen days later the hotel manager notified Quinn that they would admit the Phillies' colored players. The Phillies went back there last spring and they'll be there next spring. Meantime, the hotel is completely integrated. The Yankees moved from St. Petersburg to Fort Lauderdale partially for the same reason, but there were other factors involved, including a beautiful new ballpark. The Cardinals moved from a downtown hotel in St. Petersburg to a motel on the beach so they could have their boys together. And it's been the same with other clubs.

As I said, it's not baseball's function to crusade or to point the finger at state laws. Our theory is that Negroes want to play in baseball and we want the very best players available anywhere. Baseball will go anywhere where we're wanted. If we can't take our Negro players into certain cities, our policy is to stay away. If they can't go into certain hotels or dining places, our policy is to stay away until they can. If this policy has been effective in desegregating these towns or hotels, it's not because we've swung a club—it's because they want baseball.

When colored boys first came into our leagues there was grumbling all around among white players. Some selfishly thought that Negroes would take away their jobs. Many came from the South and were educated and brought up on segregation. It wasn't all peaches and cream. Sam Breadon of the Cardinals came to me when Jackie first broke in and said his club was threatening to strike. Five or six key players were up in arms. That was quickly brought to a halt by me as President of the National League. When the Chicago Cubs found they had some rebels, too, the situation was handled satisfactorily by the club itself. I think the disposition of the Cardinal strike threat had a lot to do with the Cubs' surrender—it was well publicized and the publicity had an effect. I don't suppose there was a single club in the league where there wasn't resentment, palaver and heated discussion, but you know how young fellows are, popping off—none of these situations came to a real climax.

I think baseball offers a terrific example of how this kind of resentment, these objections to integration, can be handled. There's a great lesson to be learned in how we've handled this problem. When I appeared before a Senate Subcommittee in 1963 I was asked to state that from our experience it was evident that no integration legislation was needed. A senator asked me if I didn't think the problem would solve itself. I said that no legislation is needed provided you are dealing with men of good will. If those who face this problem are desirous of settling it, it can be done. But if they use an alibi, an excuse for doing nothing, if those involved are not men of good will, then legislation is necessary.

These are problems for Congress to decide, not baseball. In baseball, integration has worked because baseball wants the best players we can get—white, black, yellow, green or blue. And integration succeeds with the public because the fans want the best baseball they can get. Baseball is in integrated sport. Integrated baseball has been a success.

Whether integration will be a success in other aspects of American life is not my problem. As for the future, I think it's a matter of timing before we have Negro umpires or managers. I think there are colored players with managerial possibilities. Jackie Robinson has such possibilities; Ernie Banks is a boy of great intelligence, great baseball knowledge, great know-how. A lot has been accomplished in a relatively short time. In the foreseeable future a Negro will manage a major league club.

We've gone this far in baseball—no club has tried to block, to deter, to stop the advancement of a colored ball player. On the contrary, all have been given every encouragement to succeed. It's going to take time in a great sociological upheaval like this before all the problems are solved, all the dissenters silenced. There will be disappointments, disillusionment, dissatisfaction. It will take a lot of years before all the things that all the people demand for the people can be had. We haven't reached that happy day yet.

There has been nothing in my life to which I can point with more pride than to the progress baseball has made in this field.

10

*A*mong present-day managers are many like Leo Durocher who
ignore the color of a player's skin, judging him solely on his ability to
produce. Several consciously suppress their prejudices; the majority
have none at all. Of this latter group Ralph Houk is typical. "There
has never been a color problem on the Yankees," he says, "and there
never will be. I would not permit one to arise."

Among the managers of the Southern origin is Al Dark, who succeeded Bill Rigney in 1961 and proceeded to lead San Francisco into
third place and then to a pennant triumph in 1962. Unlike Alabaman
Bobby Bragan, who acquired tolerance through minor league experience, Dark, Oklahoma-born and Louisiana-educated, was elevated
to the managerial post from the playing ranks.

Here is how Al explains his attitude toward his dark-skinned
Giants:

Since I was born in the South I know that everyone thinks that
Southerners dislike Negroes or even being with them. This isn't true
at all. The majority of the people in the South, especially the
Christian people that I have associated with, have really and truly
liked the colored people. As for socializing with them on different
levels there is a line drawn in the South, and I think it's going to be
a number of years before this is corrected, or it may never be corrected.

The way I feel, the colored boys who are baseball players are the
ones I know best, and there isn't any of them that I don't like. When

I first played with them on the Giant ball club—Willie Mays and Monte Irvin and a boy from Cuba by the name of Ray Noble, Hank Thompson, Reuben Gomez the Puerto Rican—all these boys were, as far as I was concerned, wonderful boys and I never had any kind of trouble any way with them. In fact, I felt that because I was from the South—and we from the South actually take care of the colored people, I think, better than they're taken care of in the North—I felt when I was playing with them it was a responsibility for me. I liked the idea that I was pushed to take care of them and make them feel at home and to help them out any way possible that I could in playing baseball the way that you can win pennants.

This is the feeling I have always had; I have respected many colored fellows in the National League as far as playing baseball goes. The greatest competitor I have ever seen in my life is Jackie Robinson. He has to be one of the greatest competitors the game has ever seen. Things that happened on the baseball field showed me that he had to be one of the greatest competitors.

As far as my thoughts on integration are concerned, I'd rather stay away from it as much as possible. I think it's being handled a little wrong in that the people in the South, and I think I know them because I've lived with them, although I live in California now, I feel that too many people are trying to solve the Southerners' problems before they solve their own problems in the North. In Chicago, in New York and other cities where they're having racial problems—if these problems were solved by the Northerners or people from the West who came down South, if they would take care of their own problems first and let the Southerners work it out I know they would work it out, because there are a lot of people in the South that feel that everyone's a human being, a son of God, if they are Christians, all born equally. I feel that right now it's being handled a bit too fast. It's true that in a number of cases things have to be done in order to get something accomplished, things that might be a little fast for a certain community at this particular time.

But I know that the majority of Christian people in the South want to help any person who has Negro blood in them in any way possible because they feel like we are all born equal, we are the sons of God and in the end will all be brothers in one faith. Being a Christian, I feel that this will be solved one day in the South. But they're rushing it a little too big quick right now.

The way I run a ball club is just like the way I played. As long as a man does his job I don't care who he is. I don't pick on any one in particular. If a fellow loafs, it a fellow misses a sign, if a fell doesn't produce, it makes no difference to me what color he is. I want to win and that's why I want my players to put out. There has never been any trouble between colored boys and other players on this club during my connection with it. Colored boys have never given me any trouble as manager. I wouldn't care if I had nine colored players on the field at one time as long as they can win. I think that any ball club that wins is going to draw people, there's no doubt about it. But I will say this—we have had as many as seven in the line-up at one time and as far as I am concerned as long as the boys are out there to win, if there's nine of that kind on the club I'm going to play 'em if they're the best boys on the ball club. That is up to the organization as to how man I'm going to have of colored boys. They're going to sign up the best they can sign up. It doesn't make any difference who they are as long as they're going to win. That's all this game is. As far as I'm concerned the only fun in the game or in any sport is to win. Naturally, you've got to abide by the rules, but in professional sport it's win—you have to win.

I don't think that a ball club with colored players would change the people in Birmingham or anywhere in the South. The majority of people in the South like colored people. They consider them as human beings, but right now it's being rushed too fast. I think that if a ball club moved into Birmingham or any place in the South, just like in Houston, it would sped up integration in hotels. As far as opening the thoughts of older people down there I don't think it would help at all because the older people in the South have taken care of the Negroes. They feel they have a responsibility to take care of them. That's my opinion of how things are.

11

*M*any Negroes abandoned the Deep South for the industrial centers of the North and West during the war; others entered the armed services and never returned to the scenes of their childhood. The war was over before Bill Bruton was old enough to quit Birmingham and establish residence in Wilmington, Del., where he hoped to find work and continue his education in chemistry. Soon he discovered that there was small chance for advancement for a Negro and turned to baseball:

I was born in Panola, just a little place in Alabama with some farms around it. My parents and us three boys and four girls moved to Birmingham when I was one year old. We lived in the suburb of Ensley, about two miles from Fairfield, where Willie Mays was born. The standard of living was very low because of the menial jobs Negroes had in the two main industries, coal and steel. My father was a mason and carpenter by trade but he had to work in the mines. In digger's language he was a "loader," as was my eldest brother. We lived somewhat comfortably in a four-bedroom house, but there were many things we needed and couldn't get. It's hard to compare conditions in the South with the North unless you see both.

Yes, I lived in Birmingham until 1946. The seeds of discontent were growing there then, but we had no means of protesting, for no one would listen to us. The reason conditions are coming to light now is that Negroes can at last be heard. It was very well known that discrimination was one hundred percent in Alabama. Yet I can't recall anyone discussing the limitations placed on us. We were aware, but silent.

It was impossible not to notice the way we were discriminated against in education. I lived in the neighborhood of the Ensley high school for whites. I could see the difference between their school and ours in textbooks, library and other facilities. Considering what we Negroes had to work with, we learned a lot, for our teachers were very capable. Our chemistry laboratory equipment was entirely different from that used by whites, and the same applied to our trade shops. Let's say our equipment was minimum. Furthermore, ours was the only Negro high school in a large area, and crowded.

Few streets were paved in the Negro communities of Ensley, Westfield and Fairfield. Other conveniences were inferior or not at all. It was easy to realize that we lacked many ordinary things but hard for us to make comparisons, for we stayed where we were—in segregation. We didn't know that the white world was different.

In grade school I played baseball wherever we could clear a field. Our high school had no baseball team, only football, and I didn't play football. I couldn't even make the track team as a sprinter; my speed seemed to grow on me later on. I heard about Jackie's going in the big leagues and was deeply interested, but my boyhood baseball hero was Joe DiMaggio, and when I played the outfield I tried to pattern myself after Joe. I played because I liked to play, not with the idea of making a career of it. This is true of a lot of the successful Negro players now in baseball. We had no supervised games as in the Little Leagues and so on. We developed initiative, and most of us now play highly individual ball. In childhood we went out with bat and ball without waiting for some adult to come along and organize us. We played because we loved the game, and we still love it. In those days there was no future in baseball for us. In Ensley we organized our own team and played hard—because we liked to win. Now baseball offers an incentive to anyone with talent for it, which makes me believe that many more Negroes will become major-leaguers in the future.

I went into service in '47 and never returned to Birmingham. My mother had died in 1944 and my father remarried. While I was in service I had often visited Wilmington, Delaware, where three of my sisters were living. After the war I settled there, working a year as a laborer in a chemical factory. Conditions in Wilmington were almost as bad as they'd been in Birmingham. If there was any difference I didn't notice it. We were given the poorest-paying jobs. When layoffs occurred we were the first to go. Schools and theaters were segregated. Restaurants and downtown shops were not for us. There was one thing we could do—we could sit anywhere we pleased on a bus. I lived in Wilmington from '47 to '53. The only change was that one or two theaters integrated.

I'd like to explain what goes on in a Negro's mind under such conditions. I knew what segregation meant. I was conscious of it at all times. I knew I could do nothing individually to end it. It was there, and I suppose I was waiting for a chance to fight it. But there was no chance then. A small chapter of the NAACP was located in Wilmington but I did not belong to it.

In '47 I was living in a segregated neighborhood of about five hundred families. We boys decided we wanted to have a baseball team of our own. So we formed a semipro outfit which we called the Millside Giants. Our community was outside the city limits in one of those housing developments built during the war, but we were granted admission to the municipal league. The teams were composed of fellows who worked in the factories. We played late afternoons and Sundays and practiced hard. In the spring of '49 I had the opportunity to try out with the Philadelphia Stars of the Negro National League. I stayed with them until the training season ended, then was released. So I went back to the factory and the Millside Giants.

A scout for an independent semipro team had seen me work out with the Stars. He asked me if I wanted to play on a higher semipro level. I didn't know how to reply. I was back at work and planning to save enough to go to college on the G.I. Bill of Rights. I was still interested in chemistry, and that's what I would have majored in if I'd gone to college. Finally I accepted the offer because I knew it would be hard for a Negro to get a good job as a chemist.

My new team was white-owned and all Negro. We were called the San Francisco Cubs and were supposedly based in San Francisco, but we never played there, barnstorming all year long. Our schedule took us into the Northern states and Canada. I was no stranger to the North. I'd gone there for trips from the time I was thirteen years old, and had had a small taste of Northern freedom. The Cubs played against many whit e teams in big towns and small. We had no trouble whatsoever with opposing players. Fans would jeer at us sometimes, but sports seem to change people's ideas, and ball players are more concerned with winning than someone's skin color. While I was in Canada Bill Yancey saw me. He was working as a bird-dog scout for the Braves.

I was making $250 a month with expenses under living conditions much like those in the lower minors. We traveled by bus through unsegregated territory, staying overnight in second- or third-rate hotels, with a meal-money allowance of $3 a day. This was better than I'd been doing in Wilmington and I was having a happy time. The after-war boom was over and a lot of people didn't know what to expect next. So I accepted baseball as a career, and signed with the Braves. They sent me to Eau Claire. No Negroes had ever been in the Northern League. A Negro pitcher, Roy White, was on the team with me, and I can say that 99 percent of the people in Eau Claire welcomed us warmheartedly. Ball players in the minors usually rent furnished rooms. We couldn't find one until Marty Crowe, a basketball coach for the high school, invited us to his house. One of the restaurants the ball players patronized wouldn't serve us. And I heard that the girls in town had been warned not to walk down the streets with us. These small evidences of discrimination did not affect me.

✸

Billy Bruton became Eau Claire's hero. He led the Northern League in runs, put-outs in center field, and stolen bases with 66, batting .288. The Braves gave Billy no advice about his personal conduct, on or off the field.

I had traveled around the country enough to know that very few Negroes lived in northern Wisconsin. This created quite a challenge to me. I wasn't worried about how to handle myself. I knew what I could and could not do. All I asked for was a chance to express myself, and to play to the best of my ability.

*

At Denver in the Western League in 1951 and at Milwaukee in the American Association in 1952 Billy made rapid progress. He led the Association in hits, runs, assists and in fielding average for out-fielders. His reward was advancement to the Braves in '53, the year the Boston franchise was shifted to Milwaukee.

Milwaukee already knew Billy. Now he was a local favorite on a big-league team which was showered with adulation. He bought a three-bedroom house for his wife and children.

By the time I reached the big leagues most of the hotels in other cities had agreed that Negroes were human, too, and could be admitted as guests. On my first two trips to St. Louis I was shunted off from the Chase Hotel to the Adams and segregation, then the Chase admitted Negroes and I stayed there. Few restaurants refused to serve me. Some let me know that I wasn't welcome by giving me lousy service with the idea that if I sat through it once I wouldn't come back a second time.

I can thank baseball for giving me the right to stay in first-class hotels and eat in first-class restaurants. But the club owners should have acted sooner to protect Negro players from the things that happened in the South during spring training. It's only in the last few years that most clubs have lifted restrictions against our driving our cars in Florida for fear we'd get into trouble. I'd love to take my family South so they could enjoy the warm winter climate, but we can't get motel rooms in most places and we can't rent cottages. My wife went South with me for five springs—I arranged to rent a house by paying twice as much as it was worth. She never saw an exhibition game because she wouldn't sit in the bleachers apart from the white wives. She didn't need a suntan; they did.

There were beaches everywhere in Florida, but none where she could go with other wives. And for many springs I had to eat in the kitchens of roadside restaurants while the club was traveling by bus from town to town. In towns where we played exhibition games I had to wait for a Negro cabdriver to come along and tell me where I could get a meal. All I could ask myself was—how long would I have to suffer such humiliations?

Braves fans knew nothing about the indignities Billy suffered. His teammates accepted him for what he was, a dignified, self-controlled young man determined to excel in his profession. Even when he was baited by opposing players he kept his temper—except once:

That was on Memorial Day in 1956 and Russ Meyer was pitching for the Cubs. Three of us Braves had hit home runs off Meyer. I came to bat and the first pitch was high and inside. The second pitch hit me. I rushed to the mound, Charlie Grimm, our manager, ran out and tackled me. The umpire put Meyer out of the game and he was fined $100. I was fined $50 for almost being skulled. There was a lot of throwing at us in those days. The National League passed a rule which penalized pitchers for deliberate head-hunting, which helped stop that practice.

Milwaukee was hungry for winning ball, and Milwaukee took Billy to its collective heart. He was a Milwaukean who took pride in his adopted community, working with youth agencies, helping raise funds for the Children's Home, speaking from the pulpits of Methodist churches. His four children attended local schools without consciousness of color.

Then, on July 11, 1957, Billy chased a Texas leaguer and crashed into shortstop Felix Mantilla:

I went down. I remember feeling blood on my face. I tried to roll over to spit the blood out of my mouth. My right leg was numb. I was carried off the field. My leg was in a cast for weeks. I rejoined the club in September. We were fighting for the pennant. I felt insecure on my leg, as if it'd collapse at any moment. I missed the World Series with the Yankees. It was my biggest disappointment. I was in Oklahoma City for an operation on my knee during the Series.

✳

There were other stars on the Braves: Warren Spahn, Henry Aaron, Eddie Mathews, Joe Adcock, Lew Burdette, Wes Covington, but Milwaukee followed Bill Bruton's progress toward recovery with as much interest as the fortunes of the Braves. Patiently he exercised his leg until it regained its strength. He returned in May 1958, reduced in speed but as determined as ever to excel. That October he led off the second World Series game with a home run, and topped his team in hitting with a .412 average. In 1960 he led the National League in runs scored and triples.

And then, to Milwaukee's consternation, he was traded to the Detroit Tigers.

An extraordinary outpouring of love for Billy Bruton swept Wisconsin. The state legislature passed a resolution urging him to retain his Wisconsin citizenship. Milwaukee's business and community leaders gathered in the Hotel Schroeder, seven hundred of them, to honor him for his play and civic activities. The Governor was there—a good American hailing William Bruton as "a doctor in the science of humanity."

That winter the Wisconsin B'nai Brith granted Billy one of its three interfaith awards, the other two going to bankers. Finally, the University of Wisconsin asked Billy to become a lecturer in its extension courses. His subject was the value of physical education in the national fitness program. His schedule took him to 150 high schools during the off-season.

In 1961 Billy solidified the outer defenses of the Detroit Tigers, leading the American League in put-outs at center field. During the winter of 1961-62 he drove his car from town to town preaching the virtues of physical fitness, and, by his very presence, of tolerance in baseball.

One night I finished my lecture at a high school. I was very tired and started down the highway, looking for a motel. I saw an electric sign: VACANCIES. I went in and was about to register when the clerk said, "We have no vacancies, mister."

"Your sign says so," I said.

"I forgot to turn it off," says he.

I drove down the road until I came to an eating place. I went in and telephoned the motel.

"This is Billy Bruton—" I began.

"Oh, hello, Billy!" said the voice. "How're you doing in Detroit? We miss you, Bill. The Braves aren't the same without you."

"Do you have a room for me?" I asked.

"Sure do! Come on right over!"

I drove back, parked, went in. The clerk was behind the desk. "Gee, I'm awful sorry, Billy. I didn't recognize you before." He shoved the register at me. I shoved it back.

"Mister," I said, "I'm not staying here tonight! If I can't find another motel I'll sleep in my car! If you and your likes won't rent a room to any Negro who comes along, you can't rent one to me!"

This happened in southern Wisconsin. It taught me a lesson. Baseball is a curious anomaly in American life. It seems to have been ingrained in people in their childhood. It has done wonders for me, made me someone instead of no one. It has given me many, many good friends, my home, my good neighbors and almost anything any man can ask for. Baseball is, after all, a boy's game, and children are innocent of evil. So even adults who are prejudiced revert to their childhood when they encounter a baseball player and they react with the purity of little children. Now we players must go on and purify all of American life by spreading baseball's message of tolerance. Tolerance is not going to come by our standing still and wishing for it.

We are making some progress, thanks to the NAACP and Martin Luther King, who has won the respect of even our worst enemies. We're in a hurry now. We've waited too long. We are making people listen to us at last. Any time you make people listen, as we have done these last few years, you have a chance of convincing them that we have the same right to the amenities of life as white Americans.

*

12

The Braves' policy of developing young Negro prospects rather than raiding Negro professional leagues for veterans bore its richest fruit in Henry Aaron. Like Billy Bruton, he hailed from Alabama and broke into organized ball in Eau Claire. By 1953 rumors spread through the majors that the Braves had come up with a right-hand-hitting second baseman with the potential of Rogers Hornsby. Playing that year at Jacksonville, where the park gates had been locked against me in 1946, he led the Sally League in hits, runs, doubles, RBI's, and in batting with an average of .362.

Since then Henry has twice been the National League's batting king; in 1963 he was major league home-run champion with 44 and RBI leader with 130.

In this literal transcript he speaks for and about himself:

I was born in Mobile, which is just about as far south as you can go, and segregated to the extent that Negroes can seldom do what they want to do. I lived just south of Mobile, in a little section called Tobinville, partly Negro, partly white—of course, the Negroes had the back section of the town and the whites the front.

I was the third of nine children in our family; my father worked in the Alabama Shipyards, he was a rivet buckler when I signed up for baseball in 1951. He averaged about $45 to $50 a week in paychecks before the tax was taken out. I didn't work as a boy, but my older brother worked in a grocery store and picked up about 25 bucks a week, and my older sister made about the same doing day housework, so we averaged close to $90 a week to support eleven of us. It was a struggle, of course, but we got along pretty good. We had a little garden beside our house, and we planted little things like greens, beans, and stuff to get along on.

The job my father had in the shipyards wasn't one he could depend on every week; he was often laid off the other week. It was one of those government jobs where if it wasn't wartime a riveter couldn't depend on work consistently. I finished high school, but we kids had to walk ten miles to get there. It was a good enough school, but we had to pass by a lot of other schools to get to this school. These other schools were for whites, and we had to walk past them to get to the one supposed to be for our race. Sometimes we went by bus, but we had to get there any way we could from where we was living at, Tobinville. I was big and never experienced any trouble going through the white section, but my classmates told me that on their way to school or coming home from dances they was attacked by whites. I read in the papers in my section that some of the girls was attacked by white fellows but I never knew about such things myself.

I started playing baseball in a little recreation league they had down there, one day a week. That was after I got out of school, but I couldn't play every week because I had to work on an ice truck to help support my father and mother. I was 17, going on 18 then. I doubt seriously if I learned as much in school as if I had been white, because the facilities weren't there for us to learn. We had a lot of teachers, Negro teachers; and our library was very poor. All we had was a softball team. When I heard that Jackie Robinson had broken the color barrier I got the idea I could play professional baseball. Once one Negro got in, let's put it this way, I figured any Negro could play big-league ball. I didn't know anything about professional ball until then. All a Negro knew was that the Negro American League was equivalent to the big leagues. I never dreamed I could play big-league ball. We had two Negro teams, the Mobile Shippers and the Mobile Bears.

They weren't in the Negro American League but they were professional, because Satchel Paige pitched for them. Satch's home town was Mobile—he played there for a long time. In 1951 our Mobile team was playing the Indianapolis Clowns one Sunday, which was the only chance I had to play. The traveling secretary of the Clowns, Bunny Downs, was a scout for the Clowns. He promised he would send me a contract for the next year, which he did.

The following spring, 1952, I was with them in Buffalo, New York, and was contacted for the first time by a scout for the Boston Braves, as they was then. That year was the first year I was up North. The Clowns stuck around together after games and lived in Negro hotels. One day I went with them to a little restaurant where there was white and colored. I looked around. Heck . . . I didn't know what to do, I thought I was back South again instead of in the North. I was amazed, I'd read about it and heard about it but it was the first time I'd ever experienced integration. My mother and father, they was older people, they never discussed this segregation thing. They were satisfied, you might say, as old people were then. I didn't like segregation; my sisters and brothers didn't care for it either. As soon as I got old enough I figured I'd leave the South, and so did they. There wasn't much we could do about it at the time. We had a big family to support, we had to go to school and couldn't talk about things the way they do today in Alabama.

Dewey Griggs was the Braves' scout who scouted me—he's with Philadelphia now. He told me the Clowns was willing to sell my contract, and that Sid Pollock, who owned the Clowns, would get ten thousand dollars for it, but I wasn't to get any bonus. He said Pollock would get $500 down and $500 if I ever went to Triple-A, and the balance if I ever went to the majors, but I couldn't get a penny.

I was a little hesitant about signing with the Braves. I was a youngster and having a good time with the Clowns. No one had told me anything about what to expect, so I'd have been perfectly satisfied to play baseball with the Clowns for $200 a month. It wasn't until I got to Eau Claire, Wisconsin, that I knew the difference—I was making $650 a month then, which looked like an awful lot of money to me.

There was only one Negro family in Eau Claire, but I didn't stay with them. I stayed in the YMCA with the whites. It was very good, very, very good in the Northern League. I didn't experience anything out of the way there, any segregation at all. Wes Covington was on the team with me, and a Negro catcher, Billy Bowers, who's since retired. It was the first time I ever played with white players and quite an experience for me.

The next year I went to Jacksonville in the Sally League. Felix Mantilla and Horace Garner, who's since retired, and myself, we were the first Negro players in the Sally League. All you could read about in the papers was having Negro players down there when a few years ago they'd almost nailed the gates down in the ball park to keep Jackie Robinson out of there. The first game I played in Jacksonville was against the Boston Red Sox. When I was announced to hit, the white people wouldn't applaud us. This went on for about a month until we knew we had to win the fans over. We finally did. We heard some catcalls all around the league, even at the end of the year. We played in towns like Savannah, Macon, Birmingham—not Birmingham, I mean Montgomery. We got catcalls and people threatening us in letters in Montgomery. They'd write they were coming out to the ball park and sit in right field with a rifle and shoot us. We got all sorts of threats, but it didn't worry me. I was there to play baseball, the only thing I was concerned about. I gave the letters to my manager, Ben Geraghty, and he said he was going to give 'em to some detective. Nobody ever did shoot me, did they?

Sam Wilson, who owned the Jacksonville ball club, tried to make everything as pleasant for us as he could. We stayed at a very nice home in the Negro section, but playing in the Sally League was quite a bad experience for me. Some of the names I was called, I never had head 'em in my life, before or since . . . jigaboo . . . burr-head . . . I'd never heard down home, or maybe I heard 'em but they went in one ear and came out the other, maybe I was too dumb as a kid to get mad. I'm not hot tempered, I wouldn't think about what a fan would say to me from the stands. He could never get my temper up to where I'd go in the stands after him, but if I got those kind of calls on the street—which I never did—it might be different. I never heard anything said out of the way on our ball club or by an opposing player.

In Savannah I had just hit a home run, and the opposing pitcher, I don't know who he was, he knocked Felix down four times. Felix mumbled something at him, and both benches emptied; the catcher and the pitcher being held back from hitting Felix. The stand was getting ready to empty and they had to call policemen from the outside—they was getting ready to have a race riot. We had a lot of Negro fans in the bleachers because we were the first Negroes in the Sally League and they was about to come over to the white section and the whites was getting ready to go over to the Negro section. More and more policemen came. They stood out on the field with tommy guns, announcing on the loud-speaker that if anyone came out on the field they'd get shot—it was pretty close to a race riot. I felt bad about it. What happens on a baseball field should be strictly between the players.

I was pretty lucky that year, winning the batting championship and all that—luck is part of this game. I was picked for the league all-stars but couldn't play because I'd cut my toe. The Jacksonville owner was very generous—every time I hit a home run there'd be a twenty-dollar bill in an envelope for me. Mr. Wilson still owns the Jacksonville club in the International League—he's still very good to me with advice. Charlie Grimm was manager of the Braves when I went up there the next year. Coming out of the minors I didn't know too much about the big leagues and stayed pretty close to Billy Bruton and Jim Pendleton, who were on the team with me. I went with them to the places they ate, the places they visited in Milwaukee. They told me what to do and where not to go. Charlie Grimm didn't speak to me much; he left that up to his coaches.

I broke my ankle that September, and the next year, about May or June, Fred Haney became manager. Mr. Haney was a good manager in my books; the only thing I didn't like about his way of managing was he rode the ball players when they wasn't producing, even when they was hustling. I remember a game at the Polo Grounds, Reuben Gomez was pitching, a runner was on first base and we was getting beat. I hit a ball pretty hard right at the shortstop and Mr. Haney claimed I hadn't run the ball out. But I'd given it the best I knew; the fastest runner in the world would still have hit into a double play. I've heard it said Mr. Haney took care of me on trains in the South so I wouldn't be lonesome and that he took me to breakfasts in hotels because I wasn't likely to go there by myself. This isn't true.

I've read some newspapermen saying I was just a dumb kid from the South with no education and all I knew was to go out there and hit. They didn't know how to talk to me, then wrote I didn't know how to talk to them . . . you know how newspapermen build up a lot of stories, and they built 'em up about me, me saying this and me saying that. I got wise to 'em, but what could I do? In spring training with Milwaukee I hit a triple off Curt Simmons. Well, you know how it is in spring exhibitions, they keep bringing in pitchers after pitchers. So when one newspaperman asked me if I knew who I hit that triple off of, I sad, "No." He said, "That was Curt Simmons." And then they wrote that I didn't know who the pitcher was. Well, it didn't matter to me what pitcher I was hitting triples off of, did it? That's how that story started.

In '55 John Quinn, he was the Braves' general manager then, he invited me to spring training earlier to work out on the ankle I'd fractured the last September. The Commissioner fined me and about eight other Milwaukee players for breaking the rule that all the clubs had to start training the same day. Well, the Commissioner sent me a wire stating that I had been fined. Mr. Quinn wasn't in the camp that day so I took the envelope and put it in my locker to give it to him as soon as he arrived. Charlie Grimm was still my manager at the time; he came to me and asked me where the telegram was. I forgot I had put it in my locker. That was all there was to it. But someone, I don't know whether it was Charlie Grimm or someone else, told the newspapers that I'd thrown it away in a wastebasket. That's how stories against ball players leak out. That's how the wrong impression gets out about a ball player. I knew exactly what was going on. Someone wanted people to think that I was dumb—because I was a Negro.

There was and is no discrimination on our ball club, but notice this—we never get a room in St. Louis hotels on the outside or over the swimming pool. We're always in a blind spot looking out at some old building or some green pastures or a blank wall, so nobody can see us through a window. We never can look at people walking on the street or kids swimming in the pool. When I joined the Braves we wasn't allowed to eat in the dining room in St. Louis. We ate food in our rooms. In Cincinnati the hotel was integrated, but the city was strictly segregated. A man wants to buy a meal for himself once in a while. Bruton and I decided to eat in a place called the Cat and the Fiddle. We went there and they wouldn't serve us. So we walked all around Cincinnati and couldn't find one place that would serve Negroes.

Pitchers have knocked me down a lot, and sometimes, it goes through my head that they're throwing at me because I am a Negro. What makes me think so is that Eddie Mathews is just as much of a hitter as I am, and I've batted right behind him for nine years now and have never seen him knocked down. I've been knocked down too often. Covington used to get knocked down often, too. Bruton used to get picked on. I've seen some of the white players knocked down once in a while, but most of the time it's been the Negroes.

As for my managers, I've had Charlie Grimm, Fred Haney, Charlie Dressen, Birdie Tebbetts and Bobby Bragan. Dressen knew about our problems. So does Bobby Bragan. But the others—their attitude was "Let 'em live. Keep 'em satisfied. Let 'em live." Dressen and Bragan are different. If I got knocked down they would take my side and the next inning one of the opposing players would get knocked down. And I could go up to them and talk to them about certain things, like in the South in spring training and we would take bus trips and the Negroes couldn't eat in certain places. Dressen changed that when he got with the Braves. He ruled that if we all couldn't eat together, we couldn't eat at all. We'd keep going—everybody would have to starve.

Things happen to Negro players in the South that shouldn't happen anywhere. Felix Mantilla and myself was going from Jacksonville in 1958 to spring training in Bradenton, Florida. I had a little sports car. We got along all right until outside Tampa. I was going about 55 to 60 miles an hour and a big Buick pulled up alongside me with a white kid in it. He kept tapping my bumper in the back, so I thought he wanted to go around me, a hot rodder maybe. So I pulled over to one side. But he went in front of me at about 15 miles an hour. I thought I couldn't go that slow, so I went around him. That made him try to pass me, and he ripped the front of my car at 60 an hour. Into the ditch Felix and myself went, then swerved into the highway, cars speeding all around us—we almost got killed.

We got to the camp, and I talked to some of the guys on the club. They said, "Don't mention it to newspapermen. The NAACP will get ahold of it and there you go—"

I said, "I almost lost my life and you want me to keep it a secret?" I mentioned it to newspapermen, but they didn't print a line about it. That's the kind of things happen in the South to Negro ball players. The Braves have integrated the hotel down there. We eat now in the dining room, but behind partitions.

I don't think I've received my due in publicity or money. I've had a few magazine stories, and a few endorsements, mostly when we had a strong club in '57 and '58. A ball player felt it in his pocketbook when there was no National League team in New York, which is where the money is. When the Giants went to San Francisco I never got what I should. The fans in Milwaukee have been very good to me. They never have booed me, even when I've been in some slumps and pulled some booboos on the base paths. They've always been very courteous to me.

There's been improvement in baseball for the Negro player these last few years, but I still think a lot can be done. Take myself—I'd like to get the same treatment that the Mantles and Marises have gotten when I do as well as them. We have Mays and Robinson and myself over here in the National League. When we do well we don't get the publicity and what goes with it like they do. Mays gets more than the rest of us, but he don't get what he should be getting.

A player's got to look out for his future. I've made a good start. I have an investment company in Milwaukee with Bruton and a school-teacher, Tom Cheats. It's jelling all right and should be security for me after I get out of baseball. I've saved my money. I have four kids. We live, my wife and me, in a little country town 18 miles from Milwaukee, called Mequon. Living's been very good there. The kids go to school and don't have any trouble; they play with other kids in the town. Of course Milwaukee is a pretty good city as far as Negroes are concerned, but all places can stand improvement regardless of where you go. There's no other Negroes in Mequon but us. My wife has one friend across the street; we have other neighbors who speak to us. Baseball has done a lot for me, given me an education in meeting other kinds of people. It has taught me that regardless of who you are and how much money you make, you are still a Negro. This was proven when Willie Mays tried to buy a home in San Francisco. Gosh, white players buy homes every day in the week and you never hear anything about it, but as soon as bought one every paper in the country wrote up that Mays was buying a $90,000 home in a white section. I own my own home. I got the same kind of publicity when I bought it. My home cost a little in excess of $40,000. The papers had it up to $50,000 and $60,000, then dropped it to $30,000. Mathews bought a home the same time I did, but nobody mentioned it. Me being a Negro I was supposed not to be able to afford to buy that kind of home.

There's no discrimination in Milwaukee in stores and restaurants as far as I can see. Of course I'm recognized. As soon as they see me they say, "Oh, that's Henry Aaron!" When I take my wife out to dinner they have three or four waitresses waiting on us. But if the average Negro goes in the same places, he's the last one to be served.

Negroes have done a very good job in baseball. I wish I could do more for other Negroes, especially in Birmingham and other places down South. I was called by United Press and asked what I was going to do. I told them I would like to go to Birmingham to help but I couldn't. I had a job in baseball and a tight schedule or I would have gone.

It's going to be while before we are recognized as first-class citizens everywhere. This thing is going to be dragged out, but we're making some progress. Revered King has a good policy—you can't get anywhere with violence. You can't fight back with force—you've got to show 'em you're a little bit stronger than they are in other ways. All we want is equal rights. We want our children to go to school like other children and enjoy the things that whites have been enjoying for years and years.

My mother and father are still living. They haven't changed. They understand things better, but they're old-type people in their seventies and it's hard for people to change at their age. The old-type people are all like them. When we had segregation in spring training in Florida we—Bruton and me and the others—we were staying with a schoolteacher, believe it or not. She was making a lot of money, I don't know how much, for giving accommodation to Negro ball players. I spoke to the club when they asked me whether I was satisfied with conditions in Florida. I said, "No, I'm not. We're a ball club, and a ball club's supposed to stay together because we play together."

Well, the next year we stayed at the hotel for whites. I met our landlady on the street and spoke to her. She was kind of irritated at me because she thought I was taking money away from her. I tried to explain that we was part of the ball club and wanted to be with the club at all times and get the same things the white boys was getting. She wouldn't and couldn't understand.

It isn't a case of us wanting more. It's a case of us wanting the same, which is equality. I think President Kennedy and his brother Robert did a very good job in integrating a lot of places. They say he shouldn't have sent troops into Alabama. Well, if it's going to take troops to integrate Alabama, well, you got to have 'em there. If it takes troops to put Meredith into the University of Mississippi and troops to put these kids through school in Alabama, well, that's what the President should do. He should do anything to stop violence, like at that church where those girls were killed.

I've read some of James Baldwin's books. He is a very good author with very good ideas. I haven't read *The Fire Next Time*, but a friend of mind talked to me about it. Baldwin says we've waited long enough. Well we've been waiting all this time, my parents are waiting right now in Alabama. The whites told my parents, "Wait and things'll get better." They told me, "Wait and things'll get better." They're telling these school kids, "Wait and it'll be better." Well, we're not going to wait any longer! We're doing something about it. That's what Baldwin says. He's right.

I just wish and hope there was something I could do about this stuff down in Birmingham and lots of other places. I know Birmingham—it's one of the worst cities in the South, as Alabama is one of the worst states; and being from Alabama, Mobile, I know it is a terrible city for Negroes, too.

The last time a major league club was in Birmingham was when the Braves played the Dodgers one spring. I never heard so many curses in my life. The Dodgers had seven or eight Negro ball players, all very good. Campy, Newcombe, Joe Black, Jackie, to name a few. I don't think Jackie or Campy played the whole game, about four or five innings, that's all. And Newcombe came in in the sixth inning. I never heard such filth in my life. They wasn't giving it to us, they was giving it to Jackie and Campy and Newcombe. Just recently Jackie went down there to help, and gave it back to them.

Another time, I was barnstorming through the South after the season with Willie Mays's team, and Birmingham is Willie Mays's home town. He went into a store to get some shoes. He pulled out a hundred-dollar bill to pay for 'em. They wanted to know where he'd got a hundred-dollar bill. He told 'em his name was Willie Mays and their eyes almost popped out of their ears. Here was a guy making almost a hundred thousand a year and winning the pennant for the Giants—he had a lot of hundred-dollar bills.

If I'd been playing for a ball club in New York, I'd had some hundred-dollar bills in my pocket, too, making money on TV and endorsements. The Milwaukee ball club has been good to me, but I don't make what I should. I got fifteen-thousand-dollar raises after big years from Mr. John Quinn, but how many big years does a ball player have? It's like this—I make hits, I've had tremendous years because I work at it, I want to be on top. If I see someone do something in a game I believe I can do the same thing. That's what all we Negroes should do, try to be the best—and we will.

I try to help other Negro players. I've been in this league ten years and I know what's going on. This kid I roomed with in '63, Marto Samuel, he's from the Dominican Republic. Things that happen to colored people in this country don't go in his country. He can't adjust himself to being here. Like down in spring training, he stayed in the hotel all the time and not because he's afraid. If he can't go where he chooses, he don't want to go nowhere at all. He's a very good kid and has his own way of living. It's tough for him and other Spanish players. But most of us other Negroes, we've adjusted ourselves. We've been around in baseball for a long time. We know exactly what's happening, inside baseball and out.

*

13

*I*n St. Louis, where segregation was all but total 20 years ago, white fans cheered six Negro Cardinals in 1963 as lustily as their white teammates. Baseball led the way to desegregation of public and private facilities in the Missouri metropolis and, indeed, in most parts of that state.

Here Bill White, the Cards' hard-hitting first baseman, tells about his own experiences and states his theory of how integration can be accomplished nationally:

Lake Wood is in the northwest corner of Florida, three miles from the Alabama line, 200 or so people, mostly Negroes who are not farmers in the usual sense; they're sharecroppers who farm land for others. Our leaving there was a break for me. We went to Northern Ohio, where I was able to do much more for myself than if I'd remained South. Last year I drove my family down to my birthplace. It was a shock to see the Negro children in that part of the country. I don't think they have much kind of a future.

I was brought up in Warren, Ohio, where my father became a steel worker and my mother a clerk who still classifies materials for the Air Force. I don't know exactly what they did in Florida; that part of my life is a blank, for they have never talked to me about it. But I am sure they did what the rest of Lakewood's Negroes do today, pick cotton. I do know that my mother hoped to send me to Florida A&M when I grew up. She hoped that I would become someone's secretary or perhaps a schoolteacher. But college would have been impossible, of course, due to lack of money.

Our entire family—uncles, aunts and cousins—settled in the Youngstown-Warren area during the Depression of the mid-1930s. I was an only child and pretty well taken care of, never wanted for anything and never had to work. I went to grade school, high school and then to Hiram College. Even so, we were far from well off, but my mother insisted that I get an education—which I certainly did.

I had little if any exposure to discrimination in northern Ohio steel towns or in Cleveland, an urban area with little prejudice against Negroes. You can go into the southern part of the state with ball clubs, as I did, and have no problems in a group, but you will meet discrimination as an individual. So I can say that as a small boy and later in high school and college at no time was I aware of it. The only Negro before my time in Hiram was a football player who became a doctor after graduation. Hiram is a very liberal college and exclusive because of the high tuition fees and you have to be in the upper third of your high-school class to enter. I majored in science, because I wanted to be a doctor, too. Hiram's best students qualified for medical schools after graduation, so I studied hard.

I played first base in baseball and halfback in football. As far back as grade school I was the leader of my class, and, in fact, class president in my junior and senior years at high school. I seem to have been at or near the top of everything I did, scholastically and in athletics. The students idolized ball players, and so sports overcame many problems for such as me, as it's doing now for Negroes in pro football and baseball.

I had no ambition to play pro ball of any sort until I received an offer I could not afford to turn down. Tony Ravich, a Giants scout, said I could become a very good ball player.

I went down to Pittsburgh with Ravich and worked out with the Giants. They offered me a contract and I wheedled a small bonus out of them, the equivalent of a scholarship to medical school. My mother didn't like the idea; she had her heart set on my becoming a doctor. She signed the contract, as I was under age. The only reason

I gave up college was to have a nest egg—it costs a lot of money to study medicine and there was no other way of getting my hands on that kind of money. I planned even then to make baseball a side line, not a career. As you see, my experiences until then were much the same as if I had been white.

Hank Aaron
Photo courtesy of National Baseball Hall of Fame Library, Cooperstown, NY.

Then the Giants sent me to Danville, Virginia, and I ran headlong into segregation for the first time. I don't think I reacted too well. I didn't want to face it. I asked to be sent to St. Cloud, Minnesota, which was one classification lower, but in a more liberal climate. I was hitting .324 and my manager objected. I was the only Negro on the team and lived by myself in the Negro sections of every town on the circuit. I had to eat my meals alone. Danville, as it happened, was not the worst town in the Carolina League. I had constant trouble with baiters in Burlington-Graham, North Carolina. The more the fans gave it to me, the harder I hit the ball, so they eventually decided to leave me alone, which was a victory over bigotry.

Taking it out on the ball was, you might say, but one of the psychological effects of segregation on me. The other was—I rebelled. I yelled back at the name callers. I was only eighteen and immature. As far as the Danville team was concerned, the kids were fine to me; they were mostly from the North, and one of them, Lloyd Van Dine, became my close friend.

The following year I played in Sioux City, Iowa, in the Western League. Among the towns on that circuit, Wichita, Kansas, was the only one where Negroes were segregated. My wife's brother taught school in Wichita, and I stayed in his home. In most of the other towns I roomed with two white kids from California. I had an exceptionally good year at Sioux City, nearly 200 hits and 30 home runs— maybe because the fences were short, maybe because I felt freer.

But in Dallas and other Texas League cities in 1955 I was back under the conditions that had prevailed in the Carolina League, although not quite to the same virulent degree. There were three or four other Negroes in the league then. Fortunately, I had had some understanding managers; Andy Gilbert in Danville, Dave Garcia in Sioux City, and Red Davis in Dallas. Garcia probably took more interest in me personally than the others. Gilbert was strictly a baseball man who appraised his talent and then used it to the best advantage.

As for the Giants' policy toward Negroes at that time, in one sense they were the forerunners of the big breakthrough, after the Dodgers had set the pace. When I signed with the Giants they had a lot of very good Negro and Latin players. In fact, their best young players were colored: Orlando Cepeda, Andre Rodgers, Willie Kirkland, Jose Pagan, Julio Navarro, Willie McCovey, Ossie Virgil and Ramon Monzant—they all came up the same year. Perhaps the Giants weren't sensitive to the problems I had faced in the Carolina League. I understand that Carl Hubbell said he wouldn't send me to a minor league in the South again unless I agreed to go. Alex Pompez, who discovered many Negro prospects, was our shepherd during spring training. After we were sent out we handled ourselves as best we could. Frank Forbes, well known in Harlem, advised Negroes on the Giants. His special charge was Willie Mays.

By the time I came up to the Giants in 1956, they were well established as a liberal ball club. Leo Durocher played people, not colors. At that time I had nothing but baseball on my mind. The Giants had the best players in the organization on the big team. Bill Rigney played me every inning. He played Mays every inning and used the best available talent at all times. My only aim then was to go out there and play first base the best I knew how, no matter who managed me. I don't classify managers. If you just go out there and play, you'll be around long after three or four managers have come and gone.

In December '56 I went into the Army and missed the whole '57 National League season. I was assigned to Fort Knox, Kentucky, and played baseball there for one season, then decided to quit the team because of an incident which occurred following a game with Fort Leonard Wood. After the game the Fort Knox team went to the NCO club for sandwiches. As there were two of us Negroes on the squad we couldn't eat there and went looking for another eating place out of camp. We found one and sat down, but no one came to serve us. Finally a waitress said, "Sorry, but I can't serve you," and pointed to us two. Then she gave me that "I-don't-care-myself" thing, plus the usual "It's not me, it's the owner." Everyone got up and left. By then the boys were so hungry that they went back to the NCO club. The whites left us alone on the highway to make our way back to the post as best we could. That's why I refused to play on that club again.

I returned to the Giants for spring training in '58. Cepeda was playing first base regularly and they switched me to the outfield to show me off to Eddie Stanky, who was special procurement aide for the Cardinals and looking for a hitter, either Leon Wagner, Willie Kirkland or myself. Stanky picked me and I became a Cardinal under Solly Hemus. I started poorly, batting .191 the first month and Solly gave me special batting drills. I got along fine with him—I don't see why any player should not get along with his manager if both recognize that they have different jobs. I can say this, too—any player can take care of himself in any situation if he knows how. Take these reports about pitchers throwing at Negroes. This has never happened to me in the majors and only once in the minors. At Shreveport we had a little throwing trouble, and handled it pretty good. Ray Murray, who used to catch for Cleveland, plus Ossie Virgil, Jim Ferguson the pitcher, myself and a couple of other guys on the Dallas Club took care of the situation. Ferguson threw hard at the Shreveport batters, we slid hard, hit hard and beat their brains out on the ball field—they only won three games from us all year. We knocked 'em down at second base, tagged 'em rough—we played tough baseball. That did it—no riots, no hard feelings, just showing them up on the field.

As for St. Louis, the progress in integration there has been remarkable, considering that segregation extended to the ball park until just a few years ago. If there is any trouble today in St. Louis it's due to the juveniles, the white kids.

All the so-called accommodation laws have been adopted, FEPC laws, too. You can go anywhere you want to—in publicly owned places such as parks, swimming pools, skating rinks. I don't know about privately owned places. I wouldn't want to be seen in the dinky little neighborhood spots where a Negro is not likely to be served. I go to the good restaurants, which are integrated. Young

Negroes did it by picketing, taking the guff, getting jailed. Afterwards, the restaurant owners' association agreed to open their doors to everyone. Credit should be given, too, to the mayor, who refused to prosecute the kids who picketed. You know, 35 to 45 percent of the St. Louis population is Negro, and they vote together— which is all to the good. As a result the city of St. Louis is progressive today on civil rights. The vote, which has been denied Negroes in many parts of the South, is all important. There are four or five Negro aldermen in St. Louis. These aldermen got together and proposed a fair housing bill, open occupancy to everyone. Politically the Negroes of St. Louis are mature.

I live in the country, outside St. Louis. I was the second Negro in the section where I bought a house. Since then other Negroes have bought houses, but many of our neighbors still are white. Our relationship with the whites is unself-conscious. My next door neighbor likes fishing and we fish together. He's a hunting buff and I've become one myself. Once when I was on the road there was some trouble with the heating system in my house and he came in and fixed it. He's a lot older than I am but he'll jump over the fence and talk fish or game with me, and then baseball.

As for the Cardinal organization, all they want to know about me is—can I run? Hit? And field? St. Louis baseball writers have been more than fair. Of course, every ball player thinks he should get a better press. In my case there has never been any reference to my being a Negro.

My wife, who also comes from Warren, has excellent relations with the wives of other Cardinals. She is active in the Pinch-Hitters' Club, as the organization of players' wives is called. She did not go with me to spring training in St. Petersburg until two years ago, when we finally got decent housing. Spring training is integrated for us in St. Petersburg—we have our own motel. Actually, the whole ball club is segregated from the town, which hasn't changed much, except for two or three restaurants where Negroes can eat. The

Cardinals have overcome the problem of eating at roadside restaurants on bus trips through Florida by either taking box lunches along or having something ready to eat for everyone when we arrive at the clubhouses.

The Cardinals give me a fair shake on salary but like other Negroes I make no money on the outside except that I've been lucky. I have my own sports show on KMOX radio, a CBS station, five minutes on Saturdays. No white players has been able to book such a show. The beauty of it is that it's year-round, not one of these "We only need you in the season" things. One day I was joking with Harry Carey, who announces our games. I said, "You've got an easy job, Harry. I'd like to have a try at it." He said, "Why don't you?" So I took him up on it, auditioned and was accepted by Bob Hyland, the station manager, who put Grace Brumby, the Negro operatic singer, on his station after she was barred from competing in the contest for singers in the St. Louis Municipal Opera.

My attitude toward the general civil rights struggle? It's been hypoed by the racial things that have been happening in the South and elsewhere. Too many times you think only of yourself. When you're on top you seldom think of others. Then, suddenly, you hear about police dogs biting people; policemen manhandling women; men, women, and children being murdered—and you feel you are not doing enough. You say to yourself, "What can I do? How can I help those unlucky people? I live up here, they live down there in the heart of trouble. They have the guts to fight these things. How can I help?" I think I am an over-the-average ball player, and baseball has given me the chance to prove it. It's given me a better than average living and the promise of a career in radio-television broadcasting. I meet the kind of people who can be important to me in later life. I would have lived my life in a small world in Ohio, without much discrimination, it's true, but for baseball. Sports in general enable Negroes to avoid many injustices and to enjoy privileges that most other Negroes do not have.

There are only 500 major-leaguers. Less than 100 are Negroes. All of us feel that we should do something for those who are less lucky than we are. All of us think about the problems which face the Negro people today. Our problem as ball players is what action to take. Last winter Curt Flood went to Jackson, Mississippi, to show by his presence that we in the big leagues were solidly with those unfortunate people down there. I believe—this is my opinion for and by myself—that local leadership is the best solution. I have seen what the young Negroes of St. Louis did by rallying against discrimination. They did it without the help of anyone from outside St. Louis. I look at Atlanta and see what progress has been made there, and what Martin Luther King is doing throughout the South. King stays right there—he has the heart and courage to face danger. I could go to trouble spots—all I have to do is to pick up and leave—but I wonder what I could do when I arrived. There are many evils in Missouri which must be fought against right there in Missouri. I think each individual Negro should fight local evils in his own manner. The NAACP is a necessary institution; so is CORE and the Urban League. But this question of civil rights seems to me to be a legal question, which is where NAACP is all-important.

Our problems in baseball are legal problems, too. We need a lawyer, and have a good one in Judge Cannon. In the general field of Negro-white relations, national organizations are necessary. But once the legal fight is won, it's going to be a social fight, with NAACP, CORE and the Urban League helping to see that new laws are enforced. Let me explain more precisely what I mean: the public-accommodations laws, the unemployment laws, the open occupancy laws, have all been enacted in Missouri. They are not observed in the southern part of the state, where the resort towns are. What's the use of a law that is not enforced? The next job for us in Missouri is to fight for the rigid enforcement of these laws. There's still a lot to be done. There's a lot to be done in New York, in other cities and states all over America. This must not be a one-sided clamor. We can't keep saying, "We want . . . we want . . . we want!" We must improve ourselves in raising our children, in educating them, in maintaining the standards of right living. As Judge Parsons of Chicago said at a dinner to celebrate the 100th anniversary of the Emancipation Proclamation, "We Negroes want certain rights and we're going to get them, but we must stop the jive talk, stop hanging out on street corners, stop wasting our time and our heritage." In other words, we must better ourselves by ourselves.

Now, let's apply this to baseball. As far as I am concerned, baseball owners have treated Negroes without discrimination—the St. Louis club has never slighted me in any respect. But we do not seem to be able to get what we should in added income from the outside. There's an answer to this. Ball players, not only Negroes, should form a corporation to represent them and to make contacts for them after they retire. They should do it for themselves. Some Negro players may not think they are getting as much pay as they deserve. They should not sign contracts. Every year my general manager, Bing Devine, and I go into conference about my salary. Maybe I underestimate my own value, but when I come out I believe I am getting what is due me. Most of us Negroes who have the ability to play superior ball should also have the ability to get what we deserve in pay.

Except for my few experiences in the Southern minor leagues I've escaped the worst of discrimination, and I've been aware of our problems from the start. I've always fought to solve them. I've said many things that guys who've been in baseball long before me should have said. Many players who'd been in the league long before me never said a word about housing segregation in spring training. I can't take credit for ending it—but I did say my piece. I think that all of us in the big leagues should say and do more, even fringe players.

It sums up to this—people respect a man who says out loud whatever he thinks is right. If you have ability, no matter who you are, they'll keep you around.

✹

14

*E*rnie Banks has been the bright star of the Chicago Cubs during a decade of second-division finishes. Ernie ranks sixth among active home-run hitters and holds the highest fielding average for short-stops in the game's history.

Yet little has been published nationally about Ernie the man, his experiences off the field, and the qualities which make many big-lea-guers believe that he is qualified for the honor of becoming the first Negro manager:

There were twelve of us Bankses, seven boys and five girls; I was the oldest boy, captain of the team from the time I was six. My father worked for 25 to 30 years as a porter in a wholesale grocery estab-lishment. My mother worked as a helper in hospitals or did day work around Dallas. I spent the first seventeen years of my life in segre-gated North Dallas. The YMCA was the near the campus of the high school where I graduated. I played on YMCA and church softball teams as a boy. My father had been an amateur ball player and encouraged me to take the game seriously.

After I left school I joined the Amarillo Colts, playing shortstop or the outfield. The Colts were a semipro team that played around Amarillo at first and then booked games in western Texas, New Mexico, into Kansas and as far north as Nebraska. We traveled by car around Amarillo, then by bus, playing almost every day and two games on Sundays. We split the receipts with the home team, and each Colt usually got $5 a game. The most I earned was in Hastings,

Nebraska, where there was a big crowd and we got $15. Our pay was lower than in Class C or D white ball, but it was a lot of fun for a young fellow like me, seeing the country, going from knock-down ball parks to rodeo or fair grounds. In Texas we played Negro teams but almost everywhere else we faced white teams.

I'd been unconscious of the fact that I was being discriminated against in Texas, where my neighborhood, high school, Y, the shops, playgrounds and what have you were Negro. Even on trips with the Colts I was always among Negroes. I hoped then to go to college, major in physical education and become a teacher, but when I was nineteen I caught on with the Kansas City Monarchs. We trained in Atlanta the first year and in San Antonio the next, playing a regular league schedule and exhibition games on off days. The pay was a little higher, traveling conditions a little better. We played to large all-Negro crowds in Birmingham and Memphis and to mixed crowds elsewhere. After our last game of the '53 season at Comisky Park in Chicago I sat playing cards in our hotel with my roomie, Bill Dickey—not the Yankee catcher but one of our starting pitchers. The phone rang. It was Buck O'Neil, the Monarchs' manager. "I have some news for you two," he said. "Be in the lobby at eight tomorrow morning."

We were both quite excited, thinking that Buck had found winter jobs for us in Puerto Rico or Mexico, and we were up and in the lobby by seven the next morning. Buck put us in a cab. It wasn't until we were at the corner of Clark and Addison Streets and I saw Wrigley Field through the window that I grew suspicious. "Hey, Buck, this is where the Cubs play!" I said. "Are we working out here this morning?"

"Son," said Buck, "this is a fine ball club. They don't play night ball, you know."

I understood, and my heart stood still.

Wid Mathews, the Cubs' general manager then, signed Dickey to a contract to report to their Cedar Rapids club in the spring. Then he turned to me: "We have some great fellows on this team, Ernie. We'll

Ernie Banks
Photo courtesy of National Baseball Hall of Fame Library, Cooperstown, NY.

be glad to have you around for the ten games we play here before the season ends. Go down to Phil Cavaretta, our manager, and he'll put you in uniform."

I was jumping with joy. I rushed to a phone, called Dallas, told everyone I knew about my great luck. Then I went on the field in a Cub suit for the first time. I went 0 for 3 that day against Curt Simmons of the Phillies, but I soon quieted down and got quite a few hits, including my 24th homer of the season, 23 as a Monarch.

During spring training the Cubs went all out to coach me in long hitting. My teacher was none other than Ralph Kiner. Like me, Ralph was not a natural long hitter. He had taught himself how to pull and get distance. My father had coached me whenever he could, and of course Buck O'Neil helped me a lot, too.

It wasn't until after we began our exhibition tour that spring that I ran into my conscious conflict with discrimination. With the Colts and Monarchs I'd been solely with Negroes. On the Cubs I was one of two Negroes on an otherwise white club, the other being Gene Baker, now the Pirate coach. We'd been told we couldn't stay with the team in a downtown hotel in Mobil, so when the bus stopped in front of the bus station the others went into a nearby hotel while we waited for someone to tell us where to go. I had a sudden yen for a piece of candy and ran into the bus station. The man behind the news counter looked at me and said, "What do you want, boy?" I said, "A candy bar." He said, "Get outa here in a hurry or I'll have you put out!" "Where can I buy some candy?" I insisted. "Go to the rear where the niggers are!"

Now, it may seem strange but for the first time I honestly resented being discriminated against, when I'd been discriminated against all my life until I became a Cub. I didn't know what to do, so I went back to the bus and told Gene what had happened. "Here I'm born in Davenport, Iowa, and you come from Texas, and you know less about the South than I do," he said. I was shocked, but I got over it quick, for I was young, having a good time, and loved baseball.

Conditions were rapidly changing for the better in baseball in 1954. The Cubs' management seemed to understand that every man was entitled to equal treatment. I wish I could say the same for Dallas today. Its economic situation is better than when I was a boy and things are at a faster pace, but the schools are still segregated. Housing is much the same as in Chicago. I can afford to live in Chatham Field, a mixed area in the Eighth Ward on Chicago's South Side, which has good schools. Some progress has been made in other directions, but not enough.

Chicago fans accept ball players for what they are and do. They've been especially warm to me: I have never heard a boo from the stands, which is far different from when Jackie first played at Wrigley Field. Around the league I've had no unpleasant incidents in ball parks. Kids chase me for autographs, their parents write me many letters. Even Houston has been good to us ball players. We stay at the downtown Continental Hotel, eat there or in downtown restaurants. Many Houston people we meet do not know us as ball players, yet we get good service and when they discover who we are they are eager to talk baseball.

Yet you never know. . . . One time Gene Baker, Sam Jones and myself were at the railroad station at 63rd and Dorchester in Chicago, waiting for the train to St. Louis. We went into a little place to eat. We sat and sat; no one came. We saw a waiter heaping food on other's people's plates. We should have raised a row, but didn't. We just got up and left.

The Cubs handled desegregation correctly from the start. Wid Mathews had been with Branch Rickey in Brooklyn and knew the bad spots around the league, doing all he could to smooth things out for us Negro Cubs. We might have gone to bat against minor discrimination ourselves then, but we seem to have been concentrating more on making good and having good years. Mr. Wrigley comes down to spring training. He watches our practice sessions and is available when any of us have problems. When I injured my knee and could no longer cover ground at shortstop he assigned four or five coaches to work with me so I could take over at first base. I've been able to give one hundred percent to baseball. I think I have been paid fairly. No one has put a gun to my head and made me sign a contract I didn't want to sign. No one has ever said I wasn't used to the kind of money I wanted. When you're doing a good job on the field and let club owners know you're putting all you have into the game, you can get the pay you deserve nowadays. Willie Mays is a good example of that. If you want to get something you've got to fight for it. Nobody's really going to give you anything free.

The Cubs train in Mesa, Arizona, which is second only to Salt Lake City as a Mormon community. And you know how the Mormons are about Negroes—not a single one can become a Mormon priest. A few years ago we had a little housing problem in Mesa. We stayed at a white hotel with the team, but when we tried to bring our families to Arizona with us we couldn't rent a place for them. We brought this situation to the club's attention. They made an issue of it, threatening to move the team to another site. As a result we now bring our families to Mesa; mine has spent the last two spring training periods there. We were able to rent a house two years ago, and had an apartment in an all-white building last year. Mesa has a nice climate and a relaxed sort of living. Our being there has opened up the question of segregation in the entire area. The Chamber of Commerce and civic leaders, Mormons and all, have turned tail and are now fighting against discrimination.

Every little fight for integration may not be a big grandstand play and make the papers. The fact is we ball players do act together to help each other, not as an organized group but as things come up, and on the spot. This policy has worked out beautifully. We do this because we want out kids to have things better when they reach the age of playing baseball.

When I see something I don't like I speak out. It may seem to some that I haven't been fighting hard enough, but the fact is Negro

Cubs have gotten together, as in the Mesa situation, and changed things for the better. Before our first game in Houston I went to John Holland, our general manager, and told him that we wanted to stay in the hotel with the rest of the team. He promised that the Cubs would cancel the game if the hotel turned us down. We stayed at the hotel with the team and the game was played. You can be sure that Frank Robinson, Willie Mays, Bob Clemente and others are doing all they can to make things better for Negro recruits as they come up to the big leagues. Negro stars have a big voice today in baseball with owners, general managers, and player representatives because of their status as stars.

As a Negro I must look to my own future. The broadcasting field is wide open to white players when they retire. We should get into it. The TV networks should use Negroes as commentators, both in sports and in news. I'm planning to take a course in English and public speaking in the off-season, so I'll be prepared.

Naturally I keep abreast of what's happening to Negroes in Jackson, Birmingham, Americus, Danville, Chicago, New York, throughout this country and around the world. Negroes are fighting for their just rights. I believe in helping wherever and in every way I can. I spoke at a fund-raising drive for the NAACP youth division in Chicago during the baseball season. Ball players should do active public relations work for the NAACP, the Urban League, CORE and the other organizations which are doing so much for Negroes everywhere. We players must fight to make our own conditions better, but all of us should pitch in and do our best in the bigger fight.

15

"As Robbie goes, so go the Reds," is an old saw in Cincinnati. Frank Robinson drives furiously, slams long hits, runs with bone-bruising abandon, chases flies into concrete walls. He is the Reds' bear-down, take-charge guy whose teammates rate him as a one-man baseball gang.

In private Frank is mild mannered and easy-talking, but when his integrity is assailed he quickly flares up. A national magazine has called him "the most hated man in the majors." Frank calls himself "the aggressive kind" in explanation of his running feud with a Cincinnati sportswriter whose criticisms of himself and Vada Pinson, his boyhood friend, go against his grain.

Let Frank Robinson tell you how "segregation can change a man's character":

I was born in Beaumont, in Texas, youngest of ten. My father was a railway brakeman; my mother sometimes did housework, and my older brothers worked, too. I don't remember those days much—at five my mother took me to Oakland, California, where I had a grown sister and brother who saw to it I had clothes and baseball shoes and gloves. Mom says I played with a ball in my crib. Down in Texas my father was putting aside money to send me to college one day. I grew up in an Oakland Negro district without ever knowing what discrimination was. I was halfback on the McClymonds High School team when the coach tried to convert me into a quarterback. I said, No, I didn't want to remember all those plays, I wanted to do my stuff as I always did—in my own way.

I was tall for my age and agile. From the time I was ten or eleven George Powles, McClymonds' baseball coach, had his eye on me. Powles also coached amateur teams and put me on a junior Legion club while I was in junior high. It was a fast team that won two local championships and got into the Northwestern sand lot semifinals. Fourteen of the sixteen boys on my Legion team signed professional contracts and six on my high-school team. Powles developed big-leaguers like Vada Pinson, Curt Flood, Willie Tasby and me. It was fast company for kids—we all played ball for keeps.

Bill Mattick, a Cincinnati scout, started following me when I was fourteen. The McClymonds team had only one white boy on it. In those days I never had any dismal thoughts about being a Negro. I went where I wanted to go—to parties, dances, picnics, and got the normal honors that go to a school star. You could say that I was a normal kid in Oakland, a ball-playing fool with a future, as my coach and Mr. Mattick said. I could have been a better than average student if I'd applied myself to books. But I loved the school and hated summer vacations because my friends went off to campus or took summer jobs and left me to myself.

In my senior year the White Sox, Braves and other clubs offered me contracts. The Reds offered me $3,500—$500 below the $4,000 bonus limit of those days. I took it, not because of the money but because they said they'd send me to a lower classification league where I'd get a chance to learn the game as I wanted to learn it. Right after graduation in '53 the Reds gave me a ticket to Ogden, Utah, in the Pioneer League. I was full of ambition. I batted .348, knocked in 17 homers, and Ogden walked all over the rest of the league, winning the pennant by about twelve games.

I played third base and the outfield in Ogden, but when I was moved up to Tulsa in the Texas League in '54 Johnny Schultz, the manager, put me on second base which I'd never played. I didn't know the moves, which worried me and made me hit poorly. A few days after the season opened I made an error which cost the game. That night I was told I was being sent to Columbia in the Sally League.

Now, get this—I was eighteen, I'd had no real experience with segregation or that sort of thing. South Carolina was like enemy country. I had to ride in the back of buses, I could never find a Negro cab after games. We had three Negroes on the team. We shared one small room in a boardinghouse with no shower. We had to line up to get into the tub. I stayed in the room evenings because I couldn't go to the movie theaters in town. I just wouldn't sit up in the last row in the balcony—and I like movies. I like good clothes, too—the stores that sold 'em in Columbia wouldn't let me in. And worse, I couldn't figure out why I could do as I pleased in California and Utah, but not in South Carolina. I didn't know how to take it. I was blue, homesick, ready to quit.

One day I got mad at myself. There was one way to get out of the South—by playing the best ball I knew how. I got over the blues, bore down, began to hit. I finished the season with .336 and led the league in runs scored. That summer I barreled into second on a take-out and knocked down the second baseman. He jumped up, called me a "so-and-so nigger." I went at him. Our manager, Ernie White, and some of our players pulled me off. That started the Columbia fans getting on me. Around the Sally League, in Macon, Augusta, Montgomery, Savannah, loudmouths would nag at me from the stands. I didn't care. I let 'em nag. The Reds sent me to Puerto Rico that winter so's I'd be in shape for a trial at their Tampa camp in the spring. One day I made a long throw and pulled a muscle. The pain was like a knife jabbing me. By the time I arrived in Tampa I couldn't throw.

This was bad enough, but worse was that Tampa was as rough on Negroes as Columbia. It was watch my step every time I went on the street. Negroes couldn't go out to the jai alai fronton. At the dog track I had to go downstairs and sit so far away that the dogs looked like rabbits and the rabbits like fleas. No movies, no bowling, nothing to take your mind off a bad arm and what you'd done wrong at practice sessions or in exhibition games. Conditions haven't changed in Tampa to this day. It's downright cruel to send rookies to places like that. A kid grows up dreaming of being a big-leaguer. He gets his contract and is riding high. Then suddenly he finds himself in a place where he's expected to prove he's got guts—and what happens? He's treated like a human being by the ball club, but when he steps out of the park he's lower than a mangy dog. His spirit is broken. It's a wonder he survives.

Before spring training ended in 1955 Gabe Paul, the Reds' general manager, told me he wanted to send me back to the minors until my arm came back. A specialist was treating it. I had no kick. Mr. Paul gave me a choice—did I want to go to a club he would pick or would I prefer to return to Columbia? I decided on Columbia. Most of the local fans had been fair to me. The others had sort of goaded me into playing harder. So it was Columbia again in '55.

My arm was below par. Ernie White shifted me to first base where I wouldn't have to make long throws. The fans knew about my sore arm, but when I made errors in an unfamiliar position they got on me. Back of first base were cheap twenty-five-cent seats. The ball park was ve rysmall, first base seats were almost on top of the foul line. A bunch of hecklers would start booing or cursing me from the beginning to the end of every game. I was "nigger this" or "burr-head that." I was "lazy, shiftless, no good." One day they started to blast my mother and my ancestry in filthy language. I got red-hot mad, but controlled my temper until a fly to the outfield ended the game. A bat was on the base path. I grabbed it and dashed into the stands. Marv Williams, the other Negro on the team, raced after me and grabbed me from behind. Ernie White tried to calm down the fans who were ganging up on me. White told the ones who'd done the worst name-calling that he knew them and would have them barred from the park.

That night Marv Williams and I sat down and talked things over. I decided to quit baseball and go back to Oakland where I'd be treated like a man. I told Marv I wasn't leaving by bus with the team that night and asked him to stay with me. At first he said No, then changed his mind. It rained the next day. Sitting around in that furnished room with Marv I changed my mind. I joined the club and played in every game to the end of the season.

Baseball men should think seriously about the way Negro rookies are handicapped by segregation in Southern minor leagues. The Sally League was, and I suppose still is, a hellhole for kids of eighteen to twenty away from home for the first time, especially kids who've had freedom like I had in Oakland. Segregation changes their character, hurts their personalities, hinders their development. Negro rookies should play their first year in the North or West, even though conditions in those areas are far from perfect. It didn't help Vada Pinson to live alone in Wisconsin the year he broke in. People in Wausau never had seen a Negro. They treated Vada as if he was a freak. Vada is a fine upstanding boy with a good education. He's a credit to baseball. He deserves the best from everyone.

*

Frank crashed into the major leagues in 1956 with 38 home runs and a league-leading total of 122 runs scored. Since then he has totaled 259 home runs and 800 RBI's in eight seasons. He was the single most important factor in the Reds' 1961 pennant victory and won the National League's Most Valuable Player Award.

Frank has it made, but having it made isn't enough for him. When a newspaperman dares insinuate he isn't "playing up to the limit of his potential," he doesn't write a letter to the editor—he tells the newspaperman to his face that his prejudice is showing. Twice he has become involved in clubhouse arguments with Earl Lawson of the Cincinnati *Times-Star*, once in defense of his own reputation, once in defense of Vada Pinson's. Lawson's accounts of the disputes pictured Frank as a free-swinging hooligan, and did nothing to dispel the impression that he is unreasonably sensitive.

Frank Robinson
Photo courtesy of National Baseball Hall of Fame Library, Cooperstown, NY.

Frank is the Reds' leading base stealer. His style includes hook and fall-away slides, take-outs, hook slides with flashing spikes. On many occasions the defending infielder has picked himself up, a curse on his lips—and Frank refuses to be cursed, which results in explosions. As at McClymonds, he plays for keeps. He knows where he can play best—which is in the position most familiar to him, the outfield. When Freddie Hutchinson became the Reds' manager in 1959 he shifted Frank to first base. Frank spoke his mind, which again resulted in unfavorable publicity.

He is equally outspoken about head-hunters who awarded him the dubious honor of leading the National League four times in the painful hit-by-pitcher department:

Sure, I crowd the plate and lean over. That's my style. That way I can guard the plate and get around better on inside and outside pitches. I know some pitchers fire at me on purpose. They're never going to make me back off. When they knock me down I get up and try to kill the ball. Don Drysdale twice gave me the brush-back business under the chin in '61, then hit me on the arm. The umpires tossed him out of the game and he was fined and suspended. I made two home runs and cleaned the bases for seven RBI's that day.

Camilo Pascual hit me in the head in an exhibition game in '58. The ball struck my temple. All the time I was lying in that hospital I wondered whether I'd be afraid of curve balls when I went to bat again. I did have trouble with curve balls for a while and was batting around .250 when I stopped rolling back on my heels. When I saw one I leaned in and hit it into the seats. All of a sudden I knew I had fear licked.

❋

Licking prejudice is not a one-man job. Like other cities in the border states, Cincinnati's population is divided between liberal Northerners and Southerners from the Old Confederacy.

I could have lived in the Netherlands-Plaza Hotel where the ball clubs stayed when I was a rookie, but the rates were high for a guy on a rookie's salary and meals expensive. So I took a room in the Manse Hotel in Walnut Hills, Cincinnati's Little Harlem. Brooks Lawrence, Bob Thurman and George Crowe were on the Reds then. We lived together, stuck together, went out together and pooled what we knew about the town's discrimination, so we could keep out of trouble. Conditions in Cincinnati are pretty fair today. The fans have been okay to me. I've made my share of mistakes on the field but they never get on me. They like winning ball.

But it's impossible for a Negro to go into the open market and get a house in a good neighborhood where whites live. Real estate dealers give us the run-around with a smile, even when they know we're big-league ball players. I got married in 1960 and had to rent a house in the country. I get paid to play under pressure. I don't think I make as much as I'm worth—no Negro does except Willie Mays. In '62 I hurt my back making a catch in San Francisco. A month later I injured my chest and arm making a catch in Cincinnati. In July I broke my toe when a foul ball hit it. And I had bruises in many places from getting hit by pitched balls. But I stuck in there and didn't miss a game all year, and batted .342.

I was worn out after the season, and sick because the team finished third when we ought to have won the pennant. So I said to a writer that I felt like quitting. When salary talks began that winter the papers said I'd made that remark to force Mr. DeWitt to give me a raise. I wasn't thinking of money when I said I felt like quitting. I learned how to live without money before I went into baseball. I was seventeen and knew what it feels like to go without. There was something else on my mind. White stars with records poorer than mine are paid more than I am. Some almost double their pay in extras. There's no endorsements in Cincinnati, and few chances for a Negro to cash in on his reputation as a ball player. And ball players' careers are short.

Baseball has given me a lot of things I'd never had if I led the normal life of an average Negro. Most of all it's given me the chance to know life and to think about the strange things some people do to others to put them down. I've been so deep in baseball that I don't think enough about the issues that other Negroes have been fighting for. I have four or five years left in the game. I've never given a thought to any other kind of career. Right now, I don't see any chance to latch onto a baseball job after I retire. From what I see it's going to take time for baseball executives to get around to using the talent they have in front office, coaching and managing jobs. I play better ball when my back is up after someone's tried to knock me down. That's the way other Negroes should act—get up swinging. When I get disgusted and say I feel like quitting, it just means I'm getting ready to hit the ball out of the lot.

16

The change in Dodger ownership from Mr. Rickey to Walter P. O'Malley in 1951 made little if any difference in the club's over-all attitude toward Negroes. The elaborate farm and scouting systems organized by Mr. Rickey continued to function as before.

I personally did not think Mr. O'Malley was as liberal in his thinking on integration as Mr. Rickey. I have grown to respect him a great deal in recent years and my wife has a sincere affection for him and Mrs. O'Malley. Today I sometimes am annoyed at criticism that is heaped his way. I must admit, however, I used to be his severest critic.

There have been many changes and many more Negroes on the Dodgers since I retired. Mr. O'Malley has finally absorbed the idea that the Negro must be recognized on merit alone, if not for more socially significant reasons. However, I still can't compare a Rickey with an O'Malley—there's no comparison there.

The condition of my legs in 1953 reduced my maneuverability at second base and I was shuttled between third and the outfield. My successor at second and my roommate was Jim Gilliam, a nine-year veteran of the Negro National League at 25. Jim won that year's Rookie of the Year Award with consistent hitting, speed on the bases and smooth fielding. Ten years later he was still a great player—he finished sixth in the balloting for the National League's 1963 MVP Award.

Jim Gilliam is the quiet kind, keenly observant, with an inexhaustible fund of baseball knowledge. According to Buzzy Bavasi, the Dodger's general manager, he will remain with the organization in an unspecified capacity after his playing days are over.

Says Jim:

You might say I was born on a ball field. There was one on the block where I lived in Nashville, and another right beside the school I went to. I grew up mostly out of doors because my father died when I was six months old, and my mother took a job in a barbecue pit to support me. We lived with my grandmother. I was playing softball at seven, and hard ball on a semi-pro team, the Crawfords, when I was fourteen. I never did anything but play ball, except one time I worked as a porter in a five-and-ten. Paul Jones, who was with the Nashville Black Vols of the Negro Southern League, offered me $150 a month.

Although I lived in a Negro neighborhood I had a lot of contacts with white boys playing ball. There was a barrier—we couldn't go to school or lunch counters together, but on the ball field we were equals. Baseball was the only way to make an honest living. I picked up $5 now and then in sand-lot games. When that offer of $150 a month came long I quit school in the twelfth grade.

In our segregated school I had learned to read and write, but not algebra or sciences and all that. Baseball gave me a chance to meet people in life, to know whites in mixed games, boys of my own age and older fellows. The Black Vols traveled as far east as Asheville, North Carolina, so I saw the world, so to speak, and what the segregated South was really like. Then the Baltimore Elite Giants offered me a contract and I went big league. George Scales, a great old-time second sacker, told me I could improve my batting if I learned to switch-hit.

Tommy Butts, the Elite Giants' shortstop, coached me on the double play and other tricks around the infield. I was a utility infielder in my first year, because I was just seventeen, but the next year I became a regular, hitting around .280, playing third and second, and became well known around the league. I wasn't a big hitter like Willie Mays or Ted Williams. I don't say I mastered this game. Nobody has.

Joe Black and I worked out with the Dodgers' Fort Worth team for a few days in Vero Beach one spring, but there were no Negroes in the Texas League then, so we were transferred to Montreal under Walter Alston. Jackie Robinson and Roy Campanella were the camp leaders at Vero. They were Negroes like me and their presence reassured me. As for the club, no one spoke to us about being Negro; all they wanted to do was to play ball.

If you ask me what I knew about discrimination at the time I signed with the Dodgers, I knew it existed in the United States, and that was all. I'd always felt that Negroes should have the same rights as everyone else, even when I was a kid in Tennessee. But no one talked about discrimination, and at that age I never thought about it. I thought baseball. Now, in Vero, I heard about discrimination in the town. But we were five miles away. We had our own cafeteria and didn't have to go in restaurants. In Montreal that season I lived in a French neighborhood, like Jackie had when he'd been a rookie there. The fans, everyone, the whole town treated me very well. There was no color line in Montreal, but as soon as I crossed the border and played in Syracuse I found a lot of prejudice, hooting and hollering, name-calling. I'd played in Baltimore with the Elite Giants, but not in the Orioles' ball park, and never heard a word about my color. But when I came there with the Royals, the fans got on me. Hearing those names I just bore down harder.

People who seem to have a lot of fun running Negroes down need to have their heads examined. Of course Negroes are accepted now in the big leagues, even in Texas, where Houston fans treat us fine. We have equal accommodations in the Sheraton-Lincoln Hotel and in its restaurants, yet Houston is still in Texas, and you know most Negroes are segregated. Texas is going to take a little time to get used to the idea that Negroes are also men outside ball parks.

Just to give you an idea of how Southerners are mixed up on this subject, if you're on a ball club with a Southerner, he wants to win, like you. He'll pull together with you. He knows there's no kidding about winning. If he knows you've been in the big leagues a long time, he treats you as a professional and nothing else. And the same goes for players on opposing teams. On the Dodgers today we go out together, black and white, to movies, parties and social affairs in Los Angeles. We play golf and other games together. We are one big team. Yet once you're outside baseball, it's watch your step, watch your step. . . .

I don't mean to say I have escaped trouble all my life. I had scuffles and fights with white kids in Nashville and in games when I was coming up. But since I've been a grown man, and especially in baseball, I haven't been reminded of what I am. Maybe it's because of the way I carry myself. I remember the hecklers in Syracuse, in Baltimore, in Birmingham and cities like that when I was coming north from camp in '53. They called us names, but heck—they were ignorant people.

I was one of the first Negroes to move into the Wilshire district in Los Angeles. I bought a duplex on Redondo Boulevard from a white fellow. I had white tenants for a long time, and a few more Negroes have moved into the neighborhood since then. That doesn't mean there's no housing problem in L.A., or in New York, for that matter. Only recently there was a big NAACP rally for Negro housing in Torrence. I realize I had no trouble buying a house because I was a Dodger. The only way to beat those ignorant people is to join the NAACP.

*

17

*U*ntil Minnie Minoso entered the Cleveland farm system at Dayton in 1948, Latin-American players in organized ball had been limited to those with white skins, among them 'Dolph Luque, the Cincinnati Reds' pitching star of the 1920s, and Mike Gonzales, the Cardinal catcher of "good field, no hit" fame. Today Latins of all shades and from half a dozen countries star in the majors. Many speak broken English, or none at all; those who are colored meet with the usual prejudice meted out to aliens and are doubly isolated from the white majority in areas where discrimination is prevalent.

Segregation comes as a shock to them, for at home they knew no color barriers. Some stay within their own Spanish-speaking communities. Others react with indignation and refuse to take second-class citizenship in the United States.

Among the latter is Vic Power. Vic came from Puerto Rico in 1950 to Drummondville, Ontario, in the Class D Provincial League, where he played every position in the field, batting .334. The Yankees bought his contract, then farmed him out to Syracuse in 1951. In 1952 he became a Kansas City Blue, leading the American Association in hits, doubles and triples, and batting .331. The following year he won the Association's batting title with a .349 mark, and was obviously ready for promotion to the five-time world champions, with whom he would be the first colored player.

Interest in Vic was intense among Yankee fans, who looked forward to a keen battle for the 1954 first-base post between him and Bill Skowron.

The battle never took place. Vic was traded to the Philadelphia Athletics before the season began. He moved with the A's to Kansas City in '55, then was traded to Cleveland and, finally, to Minnesota.

Although Vic has lived in the United States for 15 years he still speaks English in a lilt all his own:

In Arecibo I wanted to be a doctor so bad, and my father wanted me to go to school, so he wouldn't let me play baseball. After he die, I was around fourteen year old, I start playing baseball. You can call it sand-lot baseball, it was not organized, we don't have no coaching or nothing down there. We just play every day after school. My mother, she sew, she make dress, she support the family until I begin to play professional baseball. I go to high school, I graduate in 1949, but I play professional baseball in 1947 in our Puerto Rican league when I am sixteen.

My life change completely in baseball. As I say, I wanted to be a doctor in Puerto Rico, but I have no much chance the way things was. Everything change, living conditions were better in baseball, I was making money. I forgot about schooling and just want to play baseball forever.

In Puerto Rico we have some of the American players playing winter ball. Quincy Troupe, he was with Cleveland for a while in 1952, was one of the best catchers in the colored league for a long time. He wanted to take me to the Chicago American club in the colored league, but this was in 1948 and I didn't want to leave the school before graduation. I was seventeen then and I make $250 a month in the Puerto Rican league. In Puerto Rico you can life with that money pretty good.

The year after all those American players jump to the Mexican League I go to play in Mexico with Sal Maglie, Max Lanier, Mickey Owen, Danny Gardella. Then the league in Mexico, they fold up. Some of those players went to Canada to play, and Quincy Troupe, he took me to Drummondville. We play there in 1950 and the

Yankees bought my contract from Canada. Tom Greenwade, he was the one who started Mickey Mantle—he scout me, bought my contract for seven thousand dollar, and I got no part of the money, nothing. At Drummondville I hit good there, something like .334. In Puerto Rico I don't see no segregation. You can go any place you want, you can go restaurant, you can go movies, you can go anywhere, but the funny thing about it is if you go to a lot of places like bank or hotel, the white Puerto Ricans, they get the jobs. I've been around those places, San Juan, Cuba, Santo Domingo, Mexico. They never segregate me, but you don't see no colored people working for the money you need to go to nice hotel or good restaurant. Puerto Rico is the kind of country you can go anywhere if you got the money, but if you can't get the money you are segregated anyhow. They rich class, they go anywhere, but the others, they don't have the clothes, they don't have the money to go anywhere.

When I get the contract with the Yankees, I notice they are sending me to Kansas City, but they transfer me to Syracuse. They never told me why, but later on I thought maybe it's because Kansas City is like the South and they have no colored players down there. I didn't have too bad a year in '51 in Syracuse, I hit .298 and I think it's good enough for me to get a shot at spring training with the Yankees, but they never give me a chance, they send me to Kansas City the next year.

Now, first, I didn't know much about segregation; being a Puerto Rican I wasn't too much aware about segregation here in the United States. When they didn't give me a chance at spring training, I think maybe the Yankees, they got too many good players and I wait for next year. So I went to Kansas City and hit .331, and when they didn't call me up that year I thought maybe they want a left-hand first baseman to get a shot at that right-field stand in Yankee Stadium, and I hit right-hand.

But people start telling me the Yankees don't want me because I'm colored and they not ready for a colored player in Yankee Stadium. I start thinking about that. Then people start picketing the Stadium and I get aware. The next year I hit .349 at Kansas City. I led the league, the American Association. I think, now I can't miss, now I get my break. Finally, they call me and trade me to Philadelphia before spring training. And they put Bill Skowron, who hit right-hand like me on first base.

I was the first colored player in Syracuse when the Yankees sent me there in 1951. There was no discrimination on the club, but in Kansas City the next year the city was bad. I could go to no movie, no restaurant, just play my games and there was no place for me to go, just home. And home was a hotel in the colored section. I make a lot of Spanish friends, some white, but a lot of people don't like it too much that I am a colored player. They get mad at me. I remember I was hitting in the ball park .300–.350, but they boo me just the same every time I come to bat. The secretary of the ball club, he come to me and say I can't stay with the club in hotels in Louisville. That make me feel bad. I don't remember what I was getting for pay, but I know that when I come back to Kansas City and it's in the American League in 1955, I am hitting .319. I go to the general manager, he Parke Carroll and the players don't like him much. I never been a holdout, I want to play, but I say, "I hit .319, I am second in the American League to Al Kaline and ask to be paid right." And Parke Carroll, he say, I wasn't an established player, that Kaline, he been in baseball longer than me, which is not so. Being a human being I never thought people was going to be like that, making me live alone, go nowhere and get poor pay. But what can you do? You can't do nothing, except you play harder. I know that when I been in Louisville or Southern places where I been segregated I try to play harder so I can beat them. Maybe that is why I win batting championship in Kansas City in 1953—but they don't give me a trophy or anything like that. It is only when I am in the big league they recognize me, put me on the all-star team four times as a first baseman.

When I am called up to the big league in 1954, it is to

Philadelphia. I don't have no trouble there, the manager, Eddie Joost, he is a nice guy. But then Philadelphia team go to Kansas City the next year and I am there, and stories are told I go out with white people. Lou Boudreau, he is the manager there for a while, he call me to his office. He say, "Vic, I don't care if you go out with colored, Puerto Rican, Chinese, or white people. I just want you to give me three hour of baseball every day." That was real nice—I thank Lou about that. The trouble was not that I had trouble with anyone—it was that I marry a Puerto Rican girl. She's light-complexion, like Tité Arroyo. Everywhere she went with me the Kansas City people they no like it.

The police stop me a couple of time I was driving with her. They don't talk to me. They ask her what's she doing in my car. She told them, "I'm with my husband." They ask, "Who's your husband?" She told them, "Vic Power, the ball player." They just laugh and say, "Oh, this is a routine investigation," and left.

My wife and I, we used to live in the colored section, it's the only place we can live. So the police stop her and ask what she doing over there. She told them, "I live here, I live in this hotel here." They ask, "Who are you?" And they try to investigate her and find she is Vic Power's wife. Then they smile and let her go. Then they stop me three or four time when we was in my car because she is light-complexion, she got red hair, and I am dark. I get so mad I go to City Hall and talk to this guy who work in Human Relations. They ask this policeman why he stop me. He say, "They been stealing so many car. We saw this guy in this blue car and thought it was one of the stolen car." Then I get mad and told him I don't look like a thief, do I? I was driving easy, about twenty mile an hour when he stop me. So they all laugh and I go home.

I have no trouble in ball games with ball players, but in spring training it is awful—I have a bad incident one time. We were riding from Fort Myers to West Palm Beach where I used to train with Kansas City. The bus stop so we could go into the men's room at a gas station. The whole club went into the bathroom, and I was only colored one. I notice the gas attendant, he didn't like it, I could tell by the way he look at me. I come out and I bought a Coco-Cola from a machine. I took the bottle to the bus and I was sitting in the bus, and this man, the attendant, he come and is real nasty. "You not suppose to take this bottle," he say. I say, "Why not? I pay you a quarter for this bottle. Let me finish drinking this Coke." He say, "I don't want your quarter. I want the bottle back." Then the ball players, they all get mad at him, and I got mad, and cursed him. "Here, you take this bottle," I say, and call him a name. He left and we left and around ten minutes after that we were riding and up come the sheriff of the police in a car and stop the bus. This gas guy was with the sheriff. The sheriff, he say, "You are under arrest for using obscene language." And they wanted to put me in jail because of that. The players, they guard me. They say, they want to put up a bond for me. Finally, we collect money from the ball players and I pay five-hundred-dollar bond so I can go later on trial. Then they say, "You better not go back, Vic—they put you in jail for a long time in this part of the country." I say, "What kind of a country is this?" So the club took the money out of my salary to pay back the ball players, and I lose five hundred dollar for buying a bottle of Coke. They told me that it was best that way because if I go back they might kill me down there, you know, how they do.

The Kansas City club, they trade me to Cleveland and I hit .312. It is fine in Cleveland and in Tucson training. I bring my wife and family and it is very nice. I have no trouble in Cleveland, not even with pitchers. When I was coming up in the minors pitchers they throw at me every day and I was fighting every day to make them know I not afraid, but in the big league they don't throw at me much, maybe only when they get mad at me for my way of playing, catching the ball with one hand, grabbing hits away from them, they don't like it too much. But I think they don't throw at me because I'm colored. It's because I play my way, catch the ball with one hand, not to show off, I catch it so because it come natural with me, it's the way I feel. When I catch the ball with two hand I feel tied up. With one hand I catch the ball better, stretch better. If I catch with one hand and no make error I don't see why I should catch with two hand because a lot of sportwriter want me to. That's the censor around baseball, the sportwriter who want me to play their way and not the way that come natural to me. I don't showboat or things like that. I notice the people, the crowd, they like it when I play my way.

Talking about sportwriter, they can be prejudiced, too, you know. They don't show it to you when they talk to you, but they can hurt you in the paper. I know a writer in Kansas City who used to call me a showboat, he used to say that on the air, so people started yelling "showboat" at me from the stand. This guy, he didn't like me too much, I don't know why, because I never did nothing wrong to him, but every time he got a chance he give me a hard time.

My trouble was I get married to a light-skinned girl, we been married for six year, we very happy, but in places where they segregate, they don't like even though she is Puerto Rican. In Puerto Rico we are all the same, white to black, we call each other Puerto Rican. My mother is light-complexion, my father was dark. You have like Tité Arroyo, he's white; Cepeda, he's a little darker but not as dark as Clemente—we all mix together. But in Kansas City every time I take my wife to the ball park and they see me with her they say, "Oh, there's Vic Power with that white girl again." And then the writers go all around the country saying, "Power, he no good, he goes after white girl."

I have one more thing—in big league I have no complaint except I don't think I am paid what I would be if I was white. I don't kick, I don't hold out, but a lot of people, they say I am the best fielding first baseman in the American League, this a long time, and I sometimes say I no got the pay a white player like me get. In Cleveland I say this, and Jimmy Dykes, he tell the reporters, Vic Power is a clubhouse lawyer, and they put it in the paper. He was cold to me. The other managers, they treat me more warm. Jimmy Dykes, he never benched me, he keep playing me. After the papers say that, I ask him and he say he didn't say that. He say we have some clubhouse lawyers on the club, but not Vic Power. The reporters, they say to themselves, if they are clubhouse lawyers on the club it got to be Vic Power or Jim Piersall, they both open their mouth too much. In baseball I notice I have two managers who are real cold to me, Jimmy Dykes and Harry Craft. The others –Lou Bondreau, Eddie Joost, Bobby Bragan, and now Sam Mele with the Twins—they different, they treat me like anybody else. I don't say Jimmy Dykes and Harry Craft treat me cold because I am colored—there's something they don't like about me.

I started to play baseball when I was sixteen. Everything I got now come from baseball. I have three little boy now, five, three, and six months. Like I tell my wife, when they grow up I prefer them to be doctor or lawyer and not a ball player. I want them to live in the United States because I see more opportunity here. I don't want them to live in Kansas City or Baltimore or places where they won't be as American as they want to be. I want them to live in Minnesota, where I play now, where I got my own house, I got my friends, my wife has friends. I still got a house in Puerto Rico, my mother live there, she comes here to see me soon in the United States. I like progress. Whenever I see progress I want to be in it. If someone want me to help in stopping these terrible thing is discrimination, I go. If they don't let you have civil right, don't let you eat, don't let you vote, don't let you go to school, you should get mad on this. This is how I feel, Vic Power. You don't want people get killed when you fight, but you want people to respect you—the way it is in baseball. You don't see no trouble in clubhouses, and baseball open up those restaurant in hotel where we stay in Kansas City that was closed to us before.

Camilo Pasqual, he was sitting in this restaurant the other day. I walk in and try to be funny. I see the waitress and I pretend I am stranger and don't know Camilo. "Sir," I say. "Sir, can I integrate this table?" Camilo look at me like he never know me and say, "No, I don't want you around!" The waitress, she is scared, she turn white, and then Camilo laugh and I laugh, and we sit and have a lot fun, and the waitress, she laugh, too.

It is this way we act in Puerto Rico—we laugh and not get mad. Why not so in the United States?

Hector Lopez crossed Vic Power's trail at Kansas City and eventually wore the Yankee uniform denied to Vic. Hard-hitting Hector differs from Vic in background, personality and philosophy. He is a Panamanian who learned to speak English in Canal Zone schools and became acquainted with segregation in his boyhood while working in the U.S. Naval Base at Colon.

I was born in Colon and I'm still a Panamanian citizen. There's no color line in Panama, but the Canal Zone is run by the American government and is segregated. Whites live by themselves and the colored live by themselves and it's the same right through. The whites have their own commissaries, clubs and facilities everywhere. My father was a pitcher in the Republic; right now he's a cabdriver. I played amateur ball in the provinces of Panama, in Venezuela, Mexico, Puerto Rico, Guatemala, and Santo Domingo.

You see, there was a great fire down there in '41 and we had to move into the Zone to work for the Americans. I used to work in a bowling alley in a naval station after school, trying to make a living. The only difference today is they now fly two flags over the Canal Zone, ours and the American. I made about $100 a month playing ball at the start—our season down there lasts about two months and three weeks.

After I graduated out of high school in '51—I was eighteen—a ball player from Canada, Jean Picou, he played in the Provincial League, he recommended me to the general manager of the St. Hyacinthe ball club, which is in Quebec. I got $250 a month there, starting out. We went any place we wanted to go. In '53 I went to Williamsport in Pennsylvania, which was on a working agreement with the Athletic. Vic Power and I, we played on the Athletics together in Kansas City, beginning in '55. Vic told me how he was picked up by the police while he was driving around with his wife and they'd ask him who's the girl he's riding around with and all that stuff. At the time the A's had Harry Simpson and Jose Santiago and me, and most of the time we stayed together—I lived with a colored family. There was nice fellows on the ball club—Joe Di Maestri was one of the nicest fellows you'd want to meet. I was booed, but no racial booing, like with Vic.

The others, Simpson, Santiago, me, we never had such controversies as Vic, like going to the mayor about a cop calling him a thief. Vic is that kind of fellow. He likes to be himself. If they gave him a kick he complained all the time. I think Vic was in the right when he said all those things about being treated so. I was a hundred percent for Vic. He had a right to speak out for his rights. I knew exactly what I supposed was to be done and where I was supposed to go and I just kept away from the places I wasn't supposed to be. I stayed in the colored section most of the time and the only time I went downtown was when I wanted to buy a shirt or something like that. I never tried to go to movies or eat in a restaurant down there. I went along with it because there was nothing I could do at the time. I guess I was fortunate, nobody calling me names or things like that. I might have made a little kick if I'd heard things like Vic did.

I came to the Yankees in '59 and played second, third, left and right field. The first year I played third base. I hit good but I had a bad year in the field. In Kansas City they had one or two sportswriters. Here in New York they have thirteen. And you read in the papers how you feel, how you can't do this or that. The harder I tried the worse things got. I tried to do better, but everything seemed to turn out bad for me. I think Casey Stengel gave me a fair break; I played a lot of games the first year for him. The second year he platooned me and I had to wait, keep in good physical shape, to get a chance to play. With Ralph Houk, he just told me I was going to stay with the club, not to worry. That made a difference.

Other fellows may kick, but that's the way I am. I can't say anything different. I don't like not going in to eat on the road in the South, being told to go to the bus station if we want something, but there's nothing I can do. If the Yankees go on a road trip and know we can't get something to eat, they don't take us—we stay back.

There's a lot of segregation in Fort Lauderdale. I took my wife there last spring for the first time. She's a Panamanian and don't like it because there's a lot of places she wants to go but she's afraid to go in there, on account of this thing in the South. So she only stayed for a couple of weeks and then went home. It's hard to live with discrimination. It's improving. We've been getting points across. It won't be long . . . everything will be all right. What can I do about it when I'm not a United States citizen and I'm the way I am?

✳

$\mathcal{V}$ic Power wasn't the "Yankee type." Elston Howard was. He unostentatiously broke the color line around the Yankee bench in 1955. In 1961 he succeeded Yogi Berra as first-string catcher. Two years later he became the first Negro to win the American League's Most Valuable Player Award.

Ellie is representative of the Negro big-leaguer of today and tomorrow. Fans and newsmen disregard the color of his skin. He is popular with his teammates and especially with Yankee pitchers who largely rely on him to guide them through their games.

Ellie is a favorite with Yankee writers, who often go to him for explanations of the finer points of play. However, he has seldom been quoted on his people's struggle for equality:

You see, I was an only child—my father was a schoolteacher and is now the principal of a Negro high school in New Madrid, Missouri. During my grammar-school days my parents were divorced and my mother remarried. My stepfather is a welder. We were in the middle class, very comfortably off. In fact, I never knew anything like poverty. We had a four bedroom house when I was in school, and my stepfather and mother now live in a split-level home that I bought for them with my World Series shares.

I went from stickball, softball, and court ball to all sports in Cashon High School, where I became a four-letter man. The Kansas City Monarchs made me an offer when I was twenty, and after a debate at home I gave up the idea of college, which is why I am in baseball today.

If I hadn't gone into baseball I could have entered a Big Ten college—Michigan State, Illinois, or any one of the many Negro colleges that offered me athletic scholarships. I was an end in football, forward and center in basketball. I made all-state honors three years in a row and national honors twice.

Many unpleasant things happened when I was a kid, so far as the race problem was concerned, but I didn't realize what they meant until I grew up and traveled around. The only time Cashon played against whites was in all-star games, and I must say we dominated the whites. Our football team was highly rated nationally; the line averaged 220 pounds. Many of the boys later went to Big Ten colleges and are holding fine jobs today around St. Louis as teachers, coaches, or in the police force.

It may be that my ideas about race come from living in a mixed area in St. Louis, with lots of Italian boys around and only three Negro families on our street. I was a real close friend of the Italian who founded a mixed Negro-Italian League. Yogi knew him well before my time—he lived around there.

I spent four days in a Cardinal tryout camp when I was eighteen. Stan Musial was there and Whitey Kurowski, and I remember that I hit two home runs in one game. The Cardinals said they would send me a letter, but I'm still waiting for it.

Johnny Neun and Tom Greenwade scouted me for the Yankees and Greenwade signed me. When I went to spring training in 1950 for the first time I couldn't live with the club in St. Petersburg hotel but no one in the Yankee organization made me conscious of my color. I played on Yankee farm clubs in Muskegon and Kansas City, and then had a big season in Montreal where I won the Most Valuable Player Award. So when I came up to the Yankees in spring training in '55 I was already one of the crowd. Many of the boys knew me and I knew them. I was used to the wise guys in the stands popping off. The only time wise guys were a personal trouble to me was traveling around the South in exhibition games when the rest of the club would go one way and I'd have to go to the other side of town to a colored hotel. The Yanks have erased that—we don't go on exhibition tours around the South and we stop in only one Southern city, Richmond. In the beginning we barnstormed through Alabama, Louisiana, Texas, and Arkansas. I've been in Alabama when I couldn't play with the team because I was Negro, and had to sit it out. It was segregated living in St. Petersburg, too. I complained to Mr. Hamey and Mr. Topping. They finally arranged for us to train in Fort Lauderdale, where everything is real nice. We all have our own living quarters, dining room, and swimming pool. Fort Lauderdale's fans are real friendly. My three kids, my wife and mother-in-law come down in the spring for a month's vacation. This is integration plus.

All this came about because a Negro doctor in St. Petersburg, Dr. Ralph Windbush, spoke up. He used to board Negro ball players—I stayed in his house three days once. He announced he wasn't going to board ball players any more and got the other Negro boardinghouse operators to refuse to take ball players in. He said it was about time the ball clubs did something about desegregating us. They did, with the result that the hotels are open to Negro players in St. Pete now.

As I say, I have always been one of the Yankee crowd. That first year Phil Rizzuto was like a father to me; he knew I felt strange and took me around with him to dinner, the movies and other places. Phil used to call me up when I was alone in my room and ask me did I want to go to a show. Eddie Lopat used to talk to me about the different Yankee pitchers and opposing hitters. Hank Bauer's locker was next to mine in the clubhouse. He showed me what to do when I wasn't sure. They were old Yankees, and that gave me a great lift. And Andy Carey, our third baseman, was just like a brother. We'd be together every day. Right now whenever we play in Los Angeles Andy calls me up and we go out together.

I can say this—I haven't run into any problems on this team whatsoever. Possibly there'd have been something if I hadn't been on

Yankee minor league clubs. But the truth is, my being a Negro doesn't matter. For instance, there was a time when the St. Petersburg Yacht Club gave breakfasts for the team. The first time I couldn't go. But the next year the Yankees put my name on the "must" list. So I integrated the yacht club, the members came up to me and said they were glad I'd come.

And as far as I know I integrated the street I lived on in Teaneck, New Jersey. Other Negroes now live on that street. I often have three of my white neighbors at the Stadium as my guests. I had no difficulty buying land for the house I built on another street. Several Teaneck organizations have called up and asked me to join.

Nearby in Englewood, they've been having trouble because the school board has zoned some schools against Negroes who want their kids to have good educations. I think such trouble is caused by real estate dealers, not by parents. Real estate dealers want to keep Negroes segregated as much as possible for reasons of their own.

As for Yankee pitchers, I work with them every day, live with them at the ball park—we're members of the same family. When they lose it hurts me as much as it hurts them. I try to understand how they feel and try to make rookies feel at home with me, like Al Downing. I treat Al the way Rizzuto and Bauer and Lopat treated me. Pitchers are my responsibility. Stan Williams, when he came from the Dodgers last year, didn't know anything about American League hitters. In spring training we talked to him—Manager Houk and me—and told him what to expect. In his first game it was up to me to make him win, knowing as I did what the other team could and couldn't hit. I called all his pitches and he won. After the last out I went to him and gave him a slap on the fanny to make him feel that he had it made. Our pitchers like me to catch 'em because we work together, think together. They know they can shake me off. If they wasn't happy it'd be another story. I like it the way things are, no arguments. On other clubs pitchers and catchers argue. I don't like arguments.

I do have arguments now and then with opposing players. One

night in Cleveland an Indian batter was hit with a pitched ball, and I thought I heard a racial remark from Jimmy Piersall. I charged him. The umpire stepped between us. Jim's one of my best friends in the game, you might say, but I went after him to scare him. He won't do it again. When a fellow called a racial remark to me in the minors or the wise guy in the stands forgot I was a human being, I sometimes felt like going into the stands after him, even right here in the majors. A Baltimore wise guy was sitting down front in the stands, doing his stuff. I went to the umpire and said, "You better tell that fellow to shut up. I'm getting tired of him. If he don't something's going to happen." The umpire told me to give no mind to it, which I did. Baltimore is a rough town. They threw bottles at Umpire Paparella the last time I was there. Baseball is not a game like that. Umpires are human, like anyone else. They throw at Roger Maris down there. I can't see that. Words can get you mad, but a bottle can slit your head open and kill you.

I'm happy with the Yankees. I'm paid well to go out and do a good job. When I'm in a Yankee uniform I never give a thought to being a Negro. Regardless of race, color, or creed, a Yankee is a Yankee.

As for what's been happening in the South and elsewhere to other Negroes, sometimes you have to realize that you can't keep 19,000,000 people down forever. The people of my race realize that the white man can't intimidate them any more. Something's got to give. I'm very fortunate, being with this club, the first Negro, and being treated like a king. I think Martin Luther King has done a wonderful job. I met him and his brother last spring at the airport in Atlanta, Georgia. I introduced myself and thanked him for the great job he's done in helping the Negro in America. If I haven't done more myself it's because I have a job here of a different kind, and I'm trying to do it half as well. Sports, baseball, they've done a lot to advance integration. Colleges have helped, too. I remember Woody Hayes, coaching down in Ohio State, saying that if colleges in the South would let Negroes play they would have better football teams.

My father never had a chance when he played sand-lot ball. Now everyone sees what Mays, Aaron, Robinson and others mean to the game. We've made ourselves wanted. And baseball helps Negro boys in another way—they can go into Little League and Babe Ruth and American Legion leagues and keep off the streets as they couldn't in St. Louis when I was a kid. Now Negro and white boys play on the same teams. When these boys grow up—it'll take a little time—they will make race problems vanish and everything will be normal in our lives.

Take this as an example of how the face-to-face business changes people: Bill Dickey comes from Little Rock, Arkansas. At the very time they were having racial trouble in Little Rock, Bill was working hard to develop me into a big-league catcher. Talk to Bill Dickey and he'll tell you that while troops were in Little Rock and the whole city torn apart so some children could go to school, one Arkansan was teaching Elston Howard, Negro, the finer points of catching. All I know about handling pitchers, captaining the Yankees from behind the plate as he used to do, I learned from Bill Dickey.

Which shows you what man-to-man meetings can do.

✻

ike Elston Howard, Earl Battey is a product of normal development in integrated baseball. He was signed by the White Sox, with whom he spent three years in the shadow of Sherman Lollar before being traded to the Washington Senators in 1960.

From 1901 until his death in 1955 Clark Griffith, that unreconstructed Virginian, had operated the Senators as a lily-white club. Calvin Griffith, his nephew, yielded to progress. Battey, the first Negro star on the Senators, found a happy baseball home when the Washington franchise was shifted to Minnesota in 1961.

I was the oldest of three brothers and seven sisters. My father was a construction foreman in Whittier, just outside metropolitan Los Angeles. He pitched for the Seventh-Day Adventist Church, and my mother, believe it or not, caught for the Nine-O ladies' team that played at church outings. We lived in a neighborhood of Mexicans, Chinese and Negroes. My first sand-lot team had just one white boy on it. There could be no such thing as segregation in a situation like that.

My original ambition was to be a newspaperman, but my parents would have had to pay my tuition at a school of journalism, which wouldn't have been easy on my father's $4,800 a year plus whatever my mother made as a nurse's helper at Los Angeles General Hospital. I was a sand-lot outfielder until our catcher got hurt. From that day to this I've worn the big mitt. When I was in the ninth grade of junior high, the school started a ball club. I was thirteen, and as I went on to finish my high-school courses, I gained six years' experience by the time I was eighteen. I could hit well and had a strong arm, so every big league team except the Yankees and Phillies made me offers. I was inclined to sign with the Dodgers because they were the first to give Negroes a crack at the majors, but a friend of mine, Clifford Prelo, advised me to go with a team that had a smaller farm system and would promote me to the majors quickly. Then Hollis Thurston of the White Sox offered me a $4,000 bonus, and I took it. I was quite a veteran at nineteen, what with Legion and Municipal League ball as well as with the Junior White Sox in the wintertime. These teams were predominantly white and Mexican.

So I never knew what segregation was until I went to Colorado Springs in the Western League in 1953. I'd read about it and thought about it but never thought I'd have to live with it, for I'd played against many white teams, had many white friends, visited their homes and they visited mine. There were three Negroes on the Colorado Springs club, Sam Hairston, Bill Pope and myself. We were not discriminated against in ball parks, but in Wichita we had to live in a Negro hotel. I thought Kansas was a liberal state, yet not one hotel in Wichita would let a Negro through its front door. The same applied to Charleston, West Virginia, in 1955. Visiting Negro players couldn't even get a drink of water in a downtown restaurant. I found a room outside Charleston, near the campus of West Virginia State College, which had just been desegregated for white students but still had a faculty that was mostly Negro. I wasn't used to segregation, and I made no attempt to buck it, avoiding theaters and other places where I might not be admitted. It was the same in Louisville, where Luke Easter and myself had to live apart from our teammates.

The White Sox took a look at me in 1956; they liked my arm and catching—I'd been tutored by Bizz Mackey, who taught Roy Campanella in the Negro league. The Sox moved me and out of the minors, used me to warm up pitchers, pinch-hit, and catch second games of double-headers for three years. Sherm Lollar gave me a fine education in big-league play. To him and Al Lopez, my manager from '56 on, I owe most of what I know today about catching. In fact, I have no complaints about the White Sox' handling of Negroes, although we were subjected to segregation in spring training, discrimination on exhibition trips from the South, and all the rest of Southern racial arrogance. Many of the Sox came from California. Among them were boys I'd been close to, like Barry Latman and Jim Landis. Yet I had to separate from them in town after town. Barry or Jim many a time would say, "Come on, Earl, let's go somewhere tonight," never thinking that there were places I couldn't go. Many a time I'd slip away to a Negro restaurant to avoid unpleasantness, just as I'd slip away on road trips by car or bus when the team stopped at a gas station rest room.

After my trade to the Senators in 1960 I became a first-string catcher at last. Washington fans were very fair, the club paid me fairly considering what little I'd done until then. But the spring training situation was just as bad as with the Sox. As for Minnesota, I'd quit baseball if I had to leave this part of the country in a trade. I live in a mixed Negro-white apartment house. My social relations with our white neighbors are of the best. The Twins are one big happy family. There is no discrimination in baseball today when it comes to ability. As for Minnesota fans, when they heard that Negroes on the Twins were discriminated against in Southern spring training, they formed a committee and demanded that the club get equal accommodations for the whole club—and the club did. Cal Griffith has paid me adequately, considering the brief time I've been a regular. I have no kick there.

The only criticism I have of the Northwest is that they put an economic squeeze on Negroes. A Negro can get a good job, but he'll be underpaid. He'll get $1.50 an hour while a white will get $2.25 for the same work. Southern whites are more familiar with the Negro problems than Northerners. Individually they can be just as friendly as far as baseball is concerned—Bubba Phillips, who's from

Mississippi, was a good friend of mine when I was on the White Sox, and I have an equal number of white and Negro friends around the league. On the Twins the fellows go out of their way to do things for me, just as I do for them.

I believe that integration would be complete in baseball if the standard of pay for Negroes, especially in the minors, were raised, and if every precaution were taken to protect Negro rookies from discrimination in spring training. I've another complaint which does not apply to ball clubs. National advertisers of such things as cigarettes, shaving creams and foods, Gillette and tobacco companies, do not use Negroes enough. We have just as short a life in the game as whites and need to make all the money we can while we can. I have nothing concrete going for me in the future. I would like to coach after I retire. I do have a small investment in an agricultural equipment company. But baseball is my life.

We've made progress in baseball but I don't believe enough is being done on the outside despite the furor. Everyone said, "Wait . . . wait . . . wait!" That's all we've been doing for nearly three hundred years, waiting. We can't wait any longer.

I agree with some Southern whites in one respect, when they say that integrated education should begin at the elementary school level. There's a drastic difference in the kind of education offered by Negro and white schools all over the country. White teaching is somewhat better than ours. The best way to avoid conflict over school integration is to begin in the lower grades and then let equality seep through the whole system as the kids grow older together.

I do not mean that the issue shouldn't have been brought up in those Mississippi and Alabama universities. Those cases proved to many Negro parents that their sons and daughters should get educations in Southern white universities whenever they apply for it, and be admitted when they qualify. Young Southern Negroes have learned that it's possible to improve yourself if you fight for your rights. There are times when the only way these problems can be solved is by crashing through barriers. Once Birmingham Negroes found they were not afraid of bodily harm, whites woke up to the fact that they'd have to do something about desegregation whether they liked it or not. They learned that they could push Negroes just so far—and then we'd fight back.

People used to talk about a Negro problem. It's a white problem—it's hard to break with white tradition, with a heritage instilled in white Southerners since they were babies. Some Southerners may change, those who are wise enough to accept the facts of life. And more than a few Negroes will fight for total integration when they find that though they're outnumbered they have allies among whites. They should speak up and not be afraid that harm will come to them. The situation North and South is changing because Negroes have banded together. I don't believe in banding together like the Black Muslims preach. The Muslims are no better than Southern whites who want to segregate themselves by segregating us. I don't think putting us in a state by ourselves will answer anything. You have to live with your fellow man, no matter what color he is.

I think President Kennedy was putting forward a greater effort to end segregation than other Presidents, especially Eisenhower. I lost faith in Eisenhower after that Little Rock incident, when he let Faubus walk all over him. Eisenhower never stood pat on any civil rights issue whereas Kennedy at least committed himself to a certain amount of civil rights. Kennedy let the public know he was for civil rights, but I don't think he moved fast or firmly enough. He did not put enough effort into pushing events forward. Baseball, along with other professional sports and the music fields, has shown how it can be done—by just doing it. Sports have done more for integration than any other sector of American life. Now Negroes are entering other fields, in science, economics, the arts.

I have a brother-in-law, Stanley Sanders, who was a heck of an athlete at Whittier College, the same school Richard Nixon went to. He could have gone into professional baseball but he has a brilliant mind, and when a Rhodes Scholarship to England was offered to him he took it. He is going into the educational field because it's open to Negroes now.

It's such things that make me optimistic about the future of total integration.

✱

$\mathcal{L}$eon Wagner makes no bones about telling the world that he's happy to be a Negro and in baseball. The big right fielder of the Cleveland Indians has a potent bat, a lively tongue and some highly individualistic opinions. He was still a Los Angeles Angel on the day he discussed his favorite topic:

I've got a different angle on this bias stuff from some. The Angels are a team that has spirit. We've got intelligent boys on the Angels— Irish, Polish, Puerto Rican, Negro. Maybe a couple of guys are down in the corner of the dugout talking about those with Polish ancestry or Italian ancestry, and somebody talks about someone's Puerto Rican ancestry or Negro ancestry. We stick up for each other regardless of race, creed or color. If someone talks to me on the racial angle, one of the others, maybe he's Canadian or Irish, says, "That's not a nice question to ask Wagner," that makes the other fellow ashamed of himself or if it don't it makes him stop and think. It isn't only the Southern fellows who make these ignorant remarks. There's Billy Moran, he's from Georgia—I love him a like a brother. He speaks with a Southern accent, but he knows there's a lot of tension down South, and he talks to me with understanding. If he likes a fellow, he likes him without thinking of his race or color, and if he don't like you, he won't associate with you. He likes me. There are white fellows on the team, he don't care for their company.

Whenever a discussion comes up about myself being a Negro I t ry to beat the other fellow to the punch with some humorous jokes that relieve the pressure around the clubhouse. I let the fellows know that I consider myself a Negro and love to be a Negro, just like they love to be Polish or Italian or Irish. I let them know I have an open mind and speak from reality, that I don't get insulted by a few names being called me, or by so-called Negro racial jokes. This relaxes the situation. This makes these fellows know they don't have to worry about placing their words exactly, and keeps up the spirit of the team. Besides, I want them to know that with the Negro people under tension and fighting for their rights in the United States and around the world, I have the courage to lead them into humorousness for the sake of the team. When they rib me because I have high cheekbones and call me Indian, I say, "I'm not Indian. I'm colored and like my colored people." I say, "I like all people, including Indians. Right here I'm playing baseball, and right here that's what I'm fighting for, equality everywhere, and most of all right on this ball club."

When Felix Torres came to the Angels I tried to be a father to him. I speak a little Spanish, picked it up in Mexico and Puerto Rico. Torres was lost here. He had a wife and couldn't get an apartment and only had two words of English: "money" and "beefsteak." I thought it about time he ought to learn—he's been in the States three or four years—but I went out and got the apartment for him.

We Angels call each other names in fun. We call Albie Pearson "Midget" because he's really short, but a heck of an athlete, in my opinion. If he was Mickey Mantle's size or my size he'd be one of the higher-paid athletes in the United States. I call Lee Thomas "Mad Dog" because he likes to kick over the water cooler when he's going bad. When Steve Bilko was with us—he's big, you know—I called him "Ha'penny's Worth" like the big strong fellow in the comics. He come to me once and say he didn't like being called "Ha'penny's Worth," and if I kept on I'd have a fight on my hands. I laughed and said to come on, I was a hundred pounds heavier than him. We call Bo Belinsky everything—some days he's incredible. We love Bo like a brother. Regardless of all the publicity he gets—he's a well-liked guy on the team.

My father worked in a factory down in Chattanooga, made about $7 a week when me and my brother and sister were kids during the Depression. My mother did housework for some wealthy white people. We lived right off the main street. After school we used to have a lot of rock fights with the white kids in the school down the hill from us. Funny thing about it, I never got to see the boys I was throwing rocks at. But we didn't have much trouble with white people—everyone knew where they stood. Colored people weren't ready to make a move at the time; they weren't organized.

When I was eight and in the second grade my father decided to go to Detroit to make money in the war factories so he could send us kids to college. I enrolled in an elementary school on the West Side of Detroit. I found the curriculum entirely different. I was amazed to see the white kids, the Polish kids, the colored kids all going to school together. This was one of the biggest thrills in my life, studying together, eating lunch together, playing together and everything. I never had any trouble with the white kids, but just about when I came to Detroit they had this racial trouble, race riots. I was too young to know what was going on the night my mother made us kids get up on a bed because she heard a lot of store glass being broke down on the corner by some white mob. After that we moved to Inkster, about fifteen miles in the suburbs of Detroit, which is where I first started to play ball. My father worked on a maintenance truck that serviced homes in Detroit and my mother worked at J.L. Hudson and other department stores, running an elevator. As soon as I was old enough to work I got into an earning situation delivering newspapers. As soon as I was sixteen I put up my age and got a job in an automobile factory, Kaiser-Fraser, as a spot welder and riveter. I got out of school at about four-thirty and went to the factory and worked until twelve at night. I was making $1.72 an hour, forty hours a week. I'd take home about $60 to $70 a week after tax and everything. I played ball weekends. I didn't go out for the high-school team until the eleventh grade, I was too intent on getting my lessons done.

In Chattanooga the schools were very strict. Most teachers would whip you for chewing gum or not concentrating on what she was saying. She'd whip kids with a ruler or switch, or if she sent you to the principal he'd whip you with a strap. The teachers did the same thing in Detroit until they ran into trouble. In Chattanooga the parents wouldn't say anything about their kids getting whipped, but in Detroit nobody wanted their kids whipped. And the kids' minds were more advanced about life in Detroit; they were freer and spoke up about getting whipped. In Chattanooga the teachers were colored, but in Detroit they were Negro and white, which made a difference.

Detroit had a lot of segregation when I came there. Most of the integrated places were well known to the colored people. The segregated places were in a predominately white neighborhood. I belonged to two or three unions while I was working. I imagine they had their own problems within their ranks. Even though I was seventeen or eighteen I was too young to understand union problems. All I knew was there was a lot of gangsterism mixed up with unions. I never knew where my money was going when it was taken out of my pay envelope. When I went out for baseball as a junior in high school I was playing in Inkster Park Tuesdays and Thursdays. A white fellow used to watch me. I thought he just liked to watch high-school games. Regardless of what I went into, football or baseball, I wanted to do better than the others because I wanted to do something besides working in an automotive factory.

I wanted to be a clean-cut fellow, not like the ordinary guys that went around stealing hubcaps and getting into gang fights. I wanted to be a doctor or a lawyer or have a good job in a factory and wear nice clothes and dark glasses and talk slick conversation. There had to be a better life than the one I had. I couldn't see myself ending up no good, as I would if I'd stayed around there.

This fellow in the park kept watching me and I didn't know he was a bird-dog scout. Then my football coach in high school, where I was a fullback and pretty good at it, he was an alumni of Tuskegee Institute down in Alabama. He recommended me for an athletic scholarship.

I only stayed at Tuskegee for three semesters. I did pretty good at my lessons. The students had to study awful hard, for Tuskegee is a highly educational college. But I didn't have any spending money in Tuskegee. So I went back to Detroit to work in a factory for spending money and nice clothes. While working again I joined a semipro team, the Inkster Panthers. That's when the bird-dog scout started scouting me again.

I was hitting the ball good—everything was a line drive, a strike-out or two, then two home runs, sometimes three a game. But I was a raw-ball swinger. One day I saw in the paper the Philadelphia Phillies was giving a tryout at Ann Arbor, University of Michigan. So I went with J.C. Hartman, who's been a utility man with the Houston Colts. I passed the running test, the throwing test, the hitting test, the time test going from first to third, and from first to home. Then in two exhibition games—we stayed overnight—I hit two home runs.

But the old Philly player who ran the camp came to me and said, "Wagner, I want to tell you I like you, you're a good prospect. But I want to be honest with you—you won't have a real chance in this organization. We don't have colored players. I'm going to recommend you to a friend of mine, Ray Lucas." I don't remember this Philly fellow's name, but I respect him for telling me the truth. Me and Hartman went back to the Panthers. I soon found out that this Lucas was the boss of the bird-dog scout who'd scouted me as a kid, and was with the Giants.

Now, while I was at the Philly tryout camp, sitting, watching other boys do the tests, a fellow came crawling up to me and whispered he was a Cleveland Indian scout, spying on us, and that he'd give me a contract. The next Sunday when I played with the Panthers this scout wasn't there. The next day, Monday, I went to work and when I came home Lucas is sitting in my living room with my old bird-dog friend from the park.

"Wagner," said Lucas, "we want you to play ball for Giants," and I said, "Sure, I'd love to do that."

It was a little hard to believe because I'd always dreamed of getting signed, and here it was! They gave me a book to show me how to play the Giants' game. I was staying with my grandmother at the time—my father and mother were separated—I ask Lucas for a bonus. I know he told me a lot of soap and baloney, saying the Giants would lose the money because I was about the age to be drafted. In a way it made sense, but I was conned easily. They could have afforded to pay a bonus. But I felt that signing was a better opportunity than tearing myself down working in a factory, looking like I was fifty when I was only twenty-five years old. If I was a white fellow I'd gotten a $50,000 or $60,000 bonus, I'm sure.

They sent me to Danville, Illinois, in the Mississippi-Ohio Valley League, which was Class D. Conditions in southern Illinois were worse than what I ran into down in Tennessee. That part of Illinois is one of the most prejudiced places in the United States. Danville wasn't too bad to me and Sherman ("Roadblock") Jones, who was on the team then too. We didn't run into trouble until we got to places like Mount Vernon and Paris and so on. People would refuse to serve us in restaurants. I don't mind it as much when a restaurant owner comes up and tells you you can't eat in his place, but when a dumb waitress ignores me, because I figure a waitress wouldn't be a waitress if she knew enough to get a better job, it makes me boil.

I had no kick about what went on inside baseball, managers and players in the Giant system. I remember one white player, Jack Elias, who came from Brooklyn, coming to us and saying if we ever got into any trouble to come to him and he'd help us. I never got into any trouble, or went looking for it. In some ball parks it was the same old curriculum, fellows calling me "Coon" and "Blackie" and stuff like that. I didn't take it as an insult. I took it that these people needed more help than me.

I'm glad the Giants sent me to D ball; I needed all the help I could get. I was nineteen then, in '54, it'd have been too much pressure on me to go higher. The Northern League where I played at St. Cloud in '55 was nice. There wasn't any colored people in town. No one discriminated against me. When I went dancing or rolling skating I had a white girl friend, and no one thought anything about it. Minnesota treats Negroes beautiful . . . beautiful. I had most of my trouble in Danville, Virginia, in the Carolina League in '56. I think that's why I hit so many home runs that year, 51 of 'em and 166 RBI's. Insults pushed me to play harder. I grew up, I grew aggressive, I tried harder to win every game. That was the one way I could fight that stuff.

At Phoenix, Arizona, in '58, after I got out of military service in '57, I wasn't a politician yet. I was a ball player, not one of those stark integrationists. When I couldn't go in a place, I didn't try to start a commotion. But as I grew older, I started thinking how silly segregation is. I realized how silly it is for grown-up white Americans to look at me and tell me to my face that I don't belong to the human race. It sounds real juvenile to me when a man says, "I don't want you to eat in the same room with me." The proof of it is that a white ball player, whether he comes from the South or not, is only too glad to eat with me, shower with me, sleep with me. The most prejudiced Southerner isn't going to come up to me in a clubhouse and call me an obnoxious name. He knows his teammates will look on him as ignorant. Even when he thinks it he keeps it quiet. A few times a ball player has called me out of my name and I've told him right there that he's too dumb to be spoken to. That straightens 'em out. On every team I've been on there's been at least one prejudiced numskull. When I finally got on the Giants there was me, Willie Mays, Willie Kirkland, Felipe Alou, Valmy Thomas, Reuben Gomez—all colored. The Giants brought me up as a pinch hitter—they had playing strength. When Bill

Rigney found a spot to put me in a game when right-handers were pitching he did. I was a pretty good hitter at the time, but my defense was erratic. I could have developed quicker if they'd realized my potential. They had so much talent around that they didn't spend much time on one fellow named Wagner. I was traded to St. Louis in December 1959 because the Giants needed Daryl Spencer and Don Blasingame in the infield, and the Cardinals were having a youth movement and I was twenty-six.

Solly Hemus was just made manager and there was a lot of pressure on him to keep his job. He played me at the start of the season and put Stan Musial on the bench temporarily. Fans were hollering how could he put Wagner in left field and leave Musial on the bench, when Musial was already in the Hall of Fame. I started off real well— I had four home runs before anyone in the league had two. After about three weeks my hitting fell off, so Hemus put Musial in left field. Musial starting hitting and there I was on the bench waiting for someone to fall down, and it certainly wasn't going to be Musial. One day Hemus called me in and said, "Well, I ain't got no place to play you. Stan's hitting good in left field. You're too good a ball player to sit around on the bench and we want to drill you to take Musial's place when he retires. We're trading you to Rochester."

That was in 1960 and Stan was still playing in 1963.

So I was sent to Rochester at the end of the year, and it was from Rochester that the Angels drafted me when the league expanded in '61.

California is America for most Negroes, though there's some trouble getting decent housing in some places. The Angels pay me good, but I think I was not paid right before then.

There've been lots of times when I've been aggravated almost to swinging at a fellow, but I have always been able to control my fists and tongue. I believe in polite fights, keeping out of situations that would endanger colored ball players. You may not hurt yourself in a public fight, but you can do harm to the young colored fellows who are coming into baseball. You see, I'm in baseball for money, not glory, but being in baseball is like having four good years of education in college. Baseball gives a colored ball player a chance to make money unlimited which he'd never had if he stayed, like I might have, in a factory. I've been able to meet good people and bad people, colored or white, in baseball. Baseball gives a colored player a big voice in helping his people. He learns to be without prejudice, that all colored people are not angels and all white people not devils. A colored ball player's big name gives him a chance to do more for his people than a top colored politician. One word from a colored player about the racial situation or what' s happening around the world to his people can play a big part in stopping all this tension.

Because I'm in baseball I don't have to worry about digging ditches when I'm old. I put the first $5,000 I earned with the Giants into a half interest in a liquor store in San Francisco that took in $8,000 a month. I got out after two years and I'm looking around now to Wall Street for some sort of investment. Me and my wife and my two-year-old daughter, we have our own house in an integrated neighborhood in Los Angeles. We don't have the same kind of problems a lot of our people have. What bugs me is that I can go to certain places and do things that my people can't. When my daughter grows up I want her to be intelligent enough to go out with whoever she pleases and to use discretion in choosing her own friends whether they're black or white.

I wish I could have the power and the money to do more for my race, moneywise and politicalwise, any way that would help so my daughter would never know what her people suffered, and could live a happy life. I want to see results. I think President Kennedy could have taken a bigger stand in the South without waiting for everything to be nice and legal, especially when little girls like my daughter are getting murdered by bombs. I don't know whether President Kennedy realized that such things are worse for our country than some of the things we'd go to war far. Sending food to foreign countries where children need it is not as good as keeping our own children alive.

All we want is equality, without violence, even if the price for freedom is going to jail for it. Lots of white people died in this country for freedom, and for land and property. Lots of Indians died for their freedom. Now it's the colored people who are fighting a war for equality for themselves, and this war isn't as bloody as some wars of the past. Isn't this what we've been taught in school?

21

*T*he new generation of Negro players is too young to remember the fuss and furor that attended my entrance into organized ball. Al Downing was six years old when I played my first game at Ebbets Field. The Yankee strikeout prodigy arrived unheralded at Yankee Stadium in 1961. He was sent down to Richmond in '62 for polishing, and returned in '63 to become a regular starter, pitching so well that he received a World Series assignment.

Al is an example of the talented young Negro who can contribute much to the nation's strength in a future free from discrimination.

I don't remember any segregation in Trenton when I was a kid and I didn't hear about it elsewhere until four or five years ago. My father was in the construction business, making about $10,000 a year, which wasn't much to support eight children and a wife on. I lived in a neighborhood with Italian and Jewish boys. We'd get up a team on our street and play boys from other neighborhoods and from the nearby housing project. I had more talent as a pitcher than anywhere else. I like to run the ball game—I'd have been a quarterback if I'd played football.

I was small, but I got confidence in myself in the Babe Ruth state tournament in New Jersey when I was fifteen and pitched a no-hitter. I had four shutouts that year and pitched two games in the Babe Ruth World Series. One tournament game was in Frederick, Maryland. The officials told us that we Negroes might eat in the hotel with the others and visit them during the day, but couldn't sleep there at night. It was a big setback for me, for I had close friends on the team who'd played behind me all summer and had gone to the shore with me many a time. That could have been a lasting shock, but I took it in stride because my teammates were real pals.

I took a straight academic course at Trenton Central High was a good student, all A's and B's. I liked European history and math. I developed a keen interest in dynasties all over Europe and in Asiatic countries. My heroes were the Lafitte brothers, the pirates—you can take just so much of Lafayette riding his big white horse. I like all-around guys—not everyone is a good guy, you know.

My baseball hero was Whitey Ford, then Warren Spahn, then Willie Mays, who'd played in Trenton when I was eight. I'd save my pennies and go to New York to see Whitey pitch, never dreaming I'd be on the same staff with him. I had other fantasies as a kid. I wanted to be a doctor or lawyer because the Jewish kids in school had high aspirations like that. But I'd always come back to baseball. My pal, Eddie Berkelheimer, said, "You're going to be a Yankee pitcher, Al, and I'm going to be the club physician." Well, here I am today on the Yankees, and Ed's taking a medical course at the University of Pittsburgh. He'll get here, too, one day. I had two no-hitters in high school, and struck out nineteen men in a game with Woodbridge. I worked hard on control and taught myself a change-up when I was sixteen. In the fall of 1960 I entered Muhlenberg College—liberal arts course: English, elementary French, math, chemistry, and so on. That summer I got on a semipro team and went with them to the national sand-lot tournament in Wichita, Kansas. While out there I also pitched against Satchel Paige's ball club and struck out twelve men, some of them Triple-A pros. I was wild that day, and afterward Satchel Paige said, "Kid, you've got good potential. You throw that ball hard, but you must get it over more consistently to be a good pitcher. I just throw my fast ball now, keep it down low around their knees. But when I get men on bases I throw my old snake, and make 'em hit it in the ground. Remember, keep that ball down!" That's what I try to do now.

Frank O'Rourke, the Yankee scout, phoned me that summer. I was on a basketball scholarship at Muhlenberg and didn't play baseball. The following fall I took an extension course at Temple University in Philadelphia, and was sick from not being able to pitch. Mr. O'Rourke called me up and asked me if I wanted to be a Yankee, and I said, "I sure do." In December Bill Yancey signed me. I won 9 and lost 1 with Binghamton by July '61, and the Yankees called me up to the Stadium. I was just twenty, and there I was with all the Yankees I'd read about or seen on television. Elston Howard helped me adjust, on and off the field. Whitey Ford sat with me on the bench or in the bull pen and tried to teach me all he knew, but I realized that all pitchers have to think for themselves. I was too inexperienced to make the Yankees that year and was sent to Richmond, where I corrected certain faults I had. So by the middle of '63 I was really ready for the majors. Everything has been perfect on the Yankees—management, players and fans.

For instance, Ellie Howard roomed with me on the road in '61, helped me relax and be my normal self. Johnny Sain, our pitching coach, spent hours with me working on my breaking ball, my poise out there on the mound, and how to keep runners close to the bags. A young ball player can get lost sometimes when he's away from home. One person has different tastes from another, but on the Yankees this doesn't seem to matter. I've made friends among the players and friends around the league, including a priest in Chicago and several new friends in Los Angeles who invited me to their houses. By the way, they're all white.

Right now I'm living in a hotel room near the Stadium. If I make much money in the future, I'll invest it, probably in real estate, and buy myself a car. Marrying? Not me. Not right now, anyhow. Naturally I think about what's been happening in the South, but I'm not an expert in such situations. I plan to sit down next fall and read about what's going on. I realize that to many young Negroes of my age I'm an example of success, I suppose. I'd like to tell such boys to finish out their educations at college, as I'm doing in the off-season. If they can't do that they should go into service in the Navy or Air Force and get technical experience, so's to be better prepared to help themselves in life. I don't think quitting school and taking any old kind of job prepares a fellow. He needs other experiences than in his home neighborhood. He should learn to control himself and not get upset when things don't go his way. I think that's my best attribute— I don't get down.

As for civil rights, different people have different ideas about such things, and there are many different kinds of people. The best thing for everybody would be to learn how to get along with everybody else, the way we do on the Yankees.

$\mathcal{B}$ig-league Negroes are aware. They are eager to help in the struggle. Many more than those in this symposium volunteered to speak for publication. Rarely did anyone decline.

Among those who did were two of the game's greatest stars, Willie Mays and Maury Wills. Both might have contributed revealing facts and offered helpful suggestions. No doubt they did not wish to stir things up.

But there's no escape, not even for Willie or Maury, from being a Negro, which is more than enough to stir things up when bigots are around.

Willie is the highest paid star in baseball. He is a certain future member of the Hall of Fame. Maury is the greatest base-runner since Ty Cobb, and perhaps faster than Ty was.

I hope Willie hasn't forgotten his shotgun house in Birmingham's slums, wind whistling through its clapboards, as he sits in his $85,000 mansion in San Francisco's fashionable Forest Hills. Or the concentration camp atmosphere of the Shacktown of his boyhood. We would like to have heard how he reacted to his liberation in baseball, and to his elevation to nationwide fame. And about his relations with his managers, coaches, fellow players and his many loyal friends, black and white.

Willie has faced from the same problems that confront every Negro. He knows Harlem's good and bad; he met with bitter opposition when he tried to rent a house in a mixed neighborhood in San Francisco. Few athletes have won such acclaim as Willie on his return to New York in 1962 for an exhibition game at Yankee Stadium, where tens of thousands blocked traffic around the ball park.

Willie is the hero of a Negro success story. What has he learned from life? We'd like to know.

Willie didn't exactly refuse to speak. He said he didn't know what to say. I hope that he will think about the Negro inside Willie Mays's uniform, and tell us one day.

Willie was scouted by the Dodgers when he was seventeen. Wid Mathews reported that he couldn't hit a curve ball and Mr. Rickey passed him up, which is how he happened to become a Giant. I wish that he had been a Dodger, not only because his tremendous play and high spirits would have made us the unbeatable team of all time, but because, if he had been a Dodger he would have learned the true meaning of equality from Mr. Rickey.

Maury Wills flatly said, "I don't want to be involved in a controversy."

Maury is involved in the greatest controversy of our times whether he likes it or not. He went on a barnstorming trip with me in his rookie days in the Dodger farm system. I didn't think he had a chance of making good in the minors then, let alone the majors. The Dodgers converted him from a pitcher into an infielder; Bobby Bragan and Pete Reiser taught him how to switch-hit. One spring he was shipped to the Tigers on a look-see basis—the Tigers neither looked nor tried to see him. For nine long years he was kicked around in the bargain basements of baseball. At one time he became so discouraged that he talked of quitting the game. Life is hell for boys who try to make it and fail. Maury stuck to it. With the help of patient teachers, he is now a success.

Has Maury forgotten his colored skin? I don't think he has or can. He is articulate. He could have given valuable advice to those less fortunate than he.

No Negro in the public eye can shilly-shally any longer. One of our most talented entertainers tried to. Patrons of record shops in the Harlems throughout the nation boycotted his discs. He about-faced, got into the struggle—and the sales of his recordings boomed. He had tried to stay neutral in order not to offend TV sponsors. Now that he is in the fight he has more TV engagements than ever before.

I have been aggressive in defense of civil rights. I shall continue to be aggressive. Aggressiveness has never hurt me in business or in any other way. I may have been denied a few opportunities, but I've balanced accounts in others.

And I can live with myself.

Negro ball players should realize that their apparent security is an illusion. They should plan ahead, think of the money they can and must save. Those who believe they can keep their mouths shut will soon discover that neutrality is impossible today. They should stand forth and be counted. They also should count their money whenever they feel like handing out hundred-dollar bills. If they are not worried about their personal future, they should think of their children and their children's children. If they have no children, they should think of the kids who clamor after their autographs today, and who will ignore them when they can no longer hit their weight or wing a ball from center field to the plate.

There used to be much talk about differences between Jackie Robinson and Roy Campanella. In Roy's early Dodger years he seemed very interested in eliminating the problems that face all Negroes. Later Roy indicated that he was more interested in Roy as an individual than what happened to Roy as a member of an oppressed minority. In our many conversations this disturbed me. I thought of him as a Negro who said to himself: "If I can open that next door I may be able to open that gate to heaven on earth."

Now, as Roy has said in these pages, he understands. The tragic accident which has confined him to a wheelchair has opened the gate to awareness.

Roy will be a power for good in the future.

Those like Roy who have freely opened their hearts and minds in these pages have done a service to their people. They agree that, as the title page says, baseball has done it, which means that integration is here.

They qualify that statement by pointing out that, although baseball has integrated them on the diamond, much must yet be done before absolute equality is attained.

Baseball, in the persons of commissioner, league presidents and owners, should bring pressure on Southern towns to end all forms of discrimination, on the penalty of cutting bait and letting local bigots swim for other dollars than theirs. Baseball should protect Negro rookies against insult, isolation and discouragement during spring training. The leagues should enact a rule demanding that local authorities provide equal accommodations and services to all players at all times.

More Negroes should be employed in club offices. The Dodgers have but one, a general clerk, and other clubs none, except in lowly positions. Without belaboring this point I know that many Negroes are qualified as private secretaries, road secretaries, statisticians, press agents, head scouts, farm supervisors, coaches and managers.

Many people believe that white athletes will not play for a Negro manager. This was proved wrong at Pasadena Junior College when those six Oklahomans and the rest of the whites on the football squad took my signals and field leadership and worked very well with me.

It was also proved to me on the Dodgers. Duke Snider, Pee Wee Reese and Gil Hodges didn't care who helped them pull out of slumps. They came to me for advice on a number of occasions. Or I would go to them and say, "Watch me today and see what I'm doing wrong."

A professional athlete will play with or for anyone who helps him make more money. He will respect ability, first, last, and all the time.

This is something that baseball's executives must learn—that any experienced player with leadership qualities can pilot a ball club to victory, no matter what the color of his skin.

Baseball, which has profited greatly both at the box office and in quality of play from Negro participation, should stop ducking the broader issue of civil rights. It certainly does not speak well for baseball to affirm that Negroes are hired only for their talent. I was hired by Mr. Rickey as the spearhead in a great crusade, and every dark-skinned player who has stepped on a diamond since 1947 has been a soldier in that crusade. You, Mr. Commissioner, are a general who doesn't know he has an army or is in a war.

When I think about my mother's problems when she worked as a sharecropper in Georgia, when I think of the advances made since then, it is quite difficult for me to realize the dangers that she and others close to me had to face, including the bestial attitudes of plantation owners. If she and other Negro women had not had the courage to withstand their advances, their lives would have been wrecked. This is an old story, of concubinage, of wives torn from husbands, of children born without a name, of sexual slavery.

I want to pay a tribute to the mothers of Negro ball players, which is also a tribute to the millions of other Negro mothers who have not yet been rescued from poverty as mine was. Think of the mothers who work their bodies to the bone that their boys may have a superior education! Think of the mothers, especially in the South, who cannot send their sons to decent grade or high schools and certainly never to college! And of those in the North whose boys roam the streets while they get down on their knees to scrub or wax other mothers' floors! These are the Negro mothers of America, heroines as worthy of veneration as Harriet Tubman or Mary Bethune.

And the wives . . . Negro ball players' wives, good wives, good mothers, good housekeepers, many studying to be dieticians, social workers, teachers, newspaperwomen, nurses—they are but a tiny minority of millions of other wives who are forced to perform menial services because their husbands were not fortunate enough to have been gifted with the ability to become professional athletes.

Those whites who scorn us, despise us, call us shiftless, immoral and inherently illiterate—the answer to their slanders is in the truth as Negroes tell it! The ball players who have spoken in these pages have told that truth. They reveal that total integration is the only cure for the disease of hatred which is afflicting our America!

PART III

The Future

Your labor is for future hours
Plough deep and straight with
all your powers!
　　　—Richard Henry Horne

23

*L*ike the indomitable man that he is, Branch Rickey refuses to yield to time. He might have retired in 1956 to his Pennsylvania farm. Instead, he became the elder statesman of the St. Louis Cardinals in 1963, keeping an eye on the present while remembering the lessons of the past and still formulating plans for the future.

Here he speaks a last word:

A lot of time has passed since Jackie Robinson's first contract was signed. Now I wish to make some observations about Negroes in baseball and out.

I once had a farm club in the little Georgia League; I had five Negroes on the Dublin club. And there was no trouble. Trouble, trouble, trouble, people go looking for trouble, saying there's going to be civil war. By Judas Priest . . . it reminds me of when we trained in Panama in '47 and I had the Brooklyn club down there. A lieutenant colonel who had charge of the locks and his sergeant would push buttons and pull levers and ships would come through. I wanted to see the ships come through and made an appointment, and Mother (Mrs. Rickey) and I went there.

The lieutenant colonel said, "Mr. Rickey, would you like to bring that ship through?"

I looked. There were a great big ship and half a dozen little ones. "That big ship?" I asked.

He said, "Yes."

"Do you mean that enormous battleship? Through here?"

"Yes."

I thought he was kidding. I kept looking and looking. "It can't be done," I said.

"It'll go through," he said.

So I sat down before the buttons and levers, and I did this, and I did that. The first thing I knew, the water began to rise and it rose and rose, and things moved, and within a few minutes the battleship began to move. I give you my word—the opening was so small that it was like passing a camel through the eye of a needle, the most son-of-a-bitching undertaking I'd ever heard of in all of my life.

"This can't be," I said to myself. "This is going to be a terrible catastrophe!"

But the big ship came on, and went through the opening, and moved steadily, slowly—it looked as if it was rubbing the sides both ways. And it went by me with the same slow, deliberate speed that integration is moving in American life today and into the future. And there was that ship, loaded to the gills, in the Atlantic Ocean, where it had just been in the Pacific, on its damnable voyage of destiny to the ports of the world.

Trouble is what they predicted, disasters—"Look what you're getting into!"

And when we got there in baseball it wasn't there!

But you've got to be sure you're right before you move ahead. Then opposition falls, like chips from the axe. And you've won the game, you're on top, just as sure as little green apples grow bigger. That's what this civil rights battle is now. It's a tempest in a teapot, but in a hell of a big teapot.

I would make no change in my policies in respect to breaking the color line if I had to do it all over again. My first problem was to find a player who would represent the finest qualities of the Negro people and, at the same time, be an athlete of the first water. I did, in Jackie Robinson. My second problem was to reconcile him and the hundreds of thousands of others, all white, with whom he would associate or before whom he would play.

My third problem was the Negro people. I anticipated the overadulation of Jackie, mass Negro attendance, gifts, awards—all natural, understandable, the reaction of people who had been down and out for years and years. And, all of a sudden, someone of their own had come into public view, with class, with distinction. "Do you mean to say," they asked me, "that we can't praise him, can't honor him?" Not so! I didn't blame 'em . . . I'd have been one of 'em too. I went to three meetings of Brooklyn Negro leaders—they were wonderful, wonderfully understanding and co-operative.

Then there was the hotel situation, Robinson's being unable to stay with the club in certain cities. Wrong! Wrong! How prevent a young man like Robinson from demanding his rights? He was direct, aggressive, the kind that stands up when he is faced with injustice and will hit you right in the snoot. It's understandable—I would be that way, too, and so would any man that's a man!

Now, as I see it today, the main complaint of Negro ball players is that integration in baseball will never be complete until there's integration everywhere—and there certainly is no integration in the Southern places they train in the spring. Some say that Negroes are happier and more comfortable in spring training being together and not going out with white boys in communities where there is obvious discrimination in spirit. There may be some who would rather be segregated in Florida than go to restaurants and other public places where the evidences of discrimination are so patent. I can understand that. But this Negro moderate, this compromiser, he is hurting his people a very great deal. There should be no compromise on the part of the Negro people in this country. That's my opinion!

There should still be improvement as regards the attitude of Negro ball players. Negro ball players represent equality of rights before the American people. They should endure discomforts and embarrassment by going into segregated places to prove that it can be done.

The average Negro is not yet up to snuff in education with the white people of this country. How could he be? He hasn't had the opportunity. All he needs is to equip himself with complete insistence that he get his rights—and no compromise!

The Negro leadership is conducting itself with perfect propriety in this struggle. Take Whitney Young, Jr. of the Urban League—where is an intellect to surpass his? Or Reverend Martin Luther King? I can name fifty outstanding minds among Negroes today, university masters, Phi Beta Kappas, they're all over the place.

The big challenge to the Negro today is to fight for the right to be equal and then to qualify as an equal. And no less important is the challenge not to compromise for less than equality.

That's the way I feel about it!